GOVERNORS STATE UNIVERSITY LIBRARY

W9-AYX-943
3 1611 00058 4232

Multiage Portraits:

Teaching and Learning in Mixed-age Classrooms

WITHDRAWN

Charles Rathbone, Ph. D.

Charles Rathbone teaches in the College of Education and Social Services at the University of Vermont. He came to UVM in 1970 after working in urban education in Syracuse, New York and completing his doctorate in teacher education at Syracuse University. He cofounded the American Primary Experience Program (APEX), a teacher education program based upon the child-centered principles of the British Primary Schools. APEX won national and international recognition in 1976 and 1977. Since then he has been a visiting scholar at the Far West Laboratory for Educational Research and Development, chair of his teacher education department, founding member of the Vermont Council of Teacher Educators, and a charter member of Vermont's Standards Board for Professional Educators. The current focus of his professional life is the movement of teacher education to field settings, a focus which continues his long standing interest in schooling that is responsive to the ways children learn. He and his wife Ann live in Burlington, Vermont with their younger children, Justin and Kyla. The older ones, Melissa and Jason, still stop by every once in a while.

Anne Bingham

Anne Bingham retired in 1993 after 27 years of teaching. For 21 of those years, she taught in the multiage primary classrooms of Shelburne, Vermont. During a half-year sabbatical to study multiage in 1987, she visited 35 classrooms, mostly in Vermont, and prepared a report used by teachers around the state. She was instrumental in establishing a network of multiage teachers in northwest Vermont. She has a master's degree in reading and language arts; has presented at a number of multiage and writing workshops; has taught a college course on writing in the elementary schools; and has published articles in Language Arts and in a book for teachers of writing. In her retirement, she plans to write and travel. She and her husband Richard love to camp and have carried their tent to Britain, Ireland, and Switzerland. They live in a house they call Heroncliff on the shores of Lake Champlain. They have three grown children.

Peggy Dorta

Peggy Dorta has been teaching in multiage classrooms for 23 years. She created and has taught a graduate course on multiage for the past five years and has also shared her experience and knowledge with undergraduate education classes, fellow educators, parent groups, and school boards. She has a master's degree in special education. "Reflection" is her favorite word. Peggy adores reading, friendships, cooking/baking, family time, and teaching. As one of five children, she believes she gained her multiage roots from her family upbringing. She and her husband Angelo, who is also a multiage teacher, have three children: Amy, a college sophomore; Michael, a middle school student; and Evan, a student in her multiage classroom. They live in Underhill, Vermont, a mountainside community near Burlington. The family shares a love of sports, Nantucket, summer, travel, their black cat, and their home.

Molly McClaskey

Molly McClaskey has been a child-centered and theme-oriented educator in Vermont for 16 years. She has worked in a variety of school and classroom settings, including grades K-5, single and multiage classrooms, as well as in rural and suburban settings. A former elementary school principal, she currently consults with teachers and their school communities on topics related to multiage teaching , supporting change within a school, and integrated curriculum. Molly has a master's degree in teacher education and has taught college-level courses on multiage classroom practice. She currently works and plays in a K-1 multiage classroom in Essex, Vermont. She is investigating new strategies in authentic assessment through a teacher-organized study group at her school. She lives in an old farm house in Charlotte, Vermont, with her husband Jonathan; children Willy, 6 and Emily, 3; and their dog Tamu. Her passions include flower gardening and teaching.

Justine O'Keefe

Justine O'Keefe has been teaching in multiage classrooms in Vermont for over 20 years. Most of her work has been with young learners , ages 5-9. At the time she wrote for *Multiage Portraits*, she was working toward a master's degree in education and visiting area schools with a math consultant from whom she learned exciting ways to engage learners in hands-on mathematical experiences. Since 1979 she has taught at the K-8 Williston Central School in Williston, Vermont. Currently Justine is a member of the four-person Discovery House team which includes 90-100 youngsters in grades 1-4. Justine presents workshops to teachers and consults with educators about creating and implementing multiage classrooms. She lives with her husband and their golden retriever in Waterbury, Vermont, in an old Victorian house with a purple door.

Multiage Portraits

Teaching and Learning in Mixed-age Classrooms

Charles Rathbone, Ph.D.

and

Anne Bingham

Peggy Dorta

Molly McClaskey

Justine O'Keefe

GOVERNORS STATE UNIVERSITY
UNIVERSITY PARK
IL 60466

Charles Rathbone wishes to acknowledge the invaluable assistance from The Ford Foundation. The study would not have been possible without the help of The Foundation.

© 1993 Charles Rathbone, Ph. D., Anne Bingham, Peggy Dorta, Molly McClaskey, Justine O'Keefe. All rights reserved.

Printed in The United States of America
98 97 96 95 94 93   6 5 4 3 2 1

Published and distributed by Crystal Springs Books
Route 202, Box 577
Peterborough, NH, 03458
1-800-321-0401   924 962¹

The pages of this book are printed on recycled paper containing a minimum of 10% post-consumer waste.

Publisher Cataloging-in-Publication Data

Rathbone, Charles.
          Multiage portraits: teaching and learning in mixed-age classrooms / Charles Rathbone and Anne Bingham, Peggy Dorta, Molly McClaskey, Justine O'Keefe.- - Ist ed. - - Peterborough, N.H.:Crystal Springs Books, 1993.
[202]p.: ill. ; cm.
Includes bibliography.
Summary: Through the eyes of a University of Vermont professor of education and four classroom teachers, the inner workings of multiage classrooms are described. Through support of The Ford Foundation, Dr. Rathbone designed a three-part qualitative research study of teaching and learning in multiage classrooms.
ISBN 0-9627389-7-2
1. Teaching. 2. Learning. 3. Nongraded schools. 4. Team learning approach in education. 5. Multiage. 6. Multigrade. 7. Grouping. I. Title.
371.302 ' 82 - - dc20

Library of Congress number is available from the publisher by request.

"Dreams," from *The Dream Keeper and Other Poems* by Langston Hughes. © 1932 by Alfred A. Knopf, Inc. and renewed 1960 by Langston Hughes. Reprinted by permission of the publisher.

Cover photos by Jerry Boling
Photos and diagrams within text by Charles Rathbone
Cover and text design by Jane Forbes
Editorial coordination by Deborah Sumner

LB 1029 .N6 M76 1993

Multiage portraits

305375

To Marion Stroud

whose respect for children,
has been a beacon for us all.
Her vision of schools as places to learn
fills these pages.

LB 1029 .N6 M76 1993

Table of Contents

Preface

I have long been fascinated with the ways in which elementary school children learn in multiage classrooms. By "multiage," I mean classrooms where children of different ages and grades are intentionally placed together, where graded distinctions are minimized, and where teaching and learning make use of the range of knowledge inherent in the group. Though I have spent a good deal of time in such classrooms over my teaching career, I never had the opportunity to reside in a such a classroom over an extended period of time. In the spring of 1990, support from The Ford Foundation enabled me to carry out this residence and seek answers to a question I've carried with me for a long time: what are teaching and learning like in the multiage classrooms of teachers who are known to be good at what they do? Support from The Society For Developmental Education has allowed me to turn the research into a book for teachers, school administrators and teacher educators.

I designed a three-part qualitative research study to seek answers to my question and each part of the inquiry looks at the question from a slightly different perspective. First, I wanted to immerse myself in a multiage classroom to develop my own understanding of how teaching and learning proceeds in such a setting. The first part of my study saw me "in residence" in Anne Bingham's K-3 multiage classroom for forty days in the spring of 1990. I tied shoelaces, zipped snowpants, watched what the children did, ate hot lunch with them, helped them with their work, talked to Anne when we could during the day, and transcribed over five hundred pages of notes. The description of Room A in Part One is a result of this residence.

I wanted to balance my observations with how several teachers of multiage classroom settings saw their own practice. I chose four teachers for whom I had a great deal of respect in terms of their classroom practice and the thought they put into their classroom practice. All were primary level teachers working in different schools. Using the methodology of story as a form of qualitative inquiry, they wrote about moments in their teaching lives that were "definitively multiage in character" and from those stories, developed a set of characteristics we could agree upon as descriptive of their multiage teaching. Part Two, the Writing Project, reports this piece of the research study.

In the same year I wrote my research proposal to Ford, I chanced across a reference to Vygotsky's zone of proximal development. It was a "drop everything" moment. I left my office and went immediately to Bailey-Howe library to follow up on the reference. I was quite taken with the clarity of Vygotsky's ideas about language and the creation of knowledge and thus used the occasion of this research to employ his writings as a third "lens" for the question of multiage learning environments. The consideration of Vygotsky is included in Part Three where findings of the first two parts of the research are brought together along with several concluding remarks on multiage practice that are wholly my own.

I am grateful to several people who played important roles in the research and publication efforts. Jim Raths first spoke with Barbara Hatton of The Ford Foundation of my interest in multiage education. Dr. Hatton, as program officer of the Education and Culture Division, recognized the promise of this research to show classroom practices that made use of student diversity. I felt her personal support as well as the institutional support she represented and I am grateful for her confidence in the work. Without her vision and Jim's encouragement, the research would not have happened.

The Society For Developmental Education has been central in the publication of this research. Jim Grant's belief in the work, Debbie Sumner's exquisite editing, and Garry Brown's commentary regarding the final details of publication have made this book a reality.

The actual research would not have been possible without the collaboration of my colleague, Anne Bingham. Her patience with my presence in Room A was stunning. She helped me to understand her world through her incisive writing, direct commentary, and her daily effort to create meaning with the children in Room A. To this must also be added an appreciation for the conscious support given Anne and me by Marilyn Johnson, Liz Farman, and Phyllis Murray, other members of Anne's team. Together, along with their principal, G. Alfred Mercaldo, their doors were open from the very first. They suffered my occasional excursion into their realms, graciously.

Peggy, Molly, Anne, and Justine's writings touch both the mind and the heart. Their "stories" are poignant reminders of just how present great teachers are in children's lives. I appreciate the time they took to work with me and their risk taking and honesty with each other and recognize what they taught me in our work together.

Anne Watson took us through our writing project step by step. Her presence allowed me to listen to the teachers in ways that would have been otherwise impossible and her skill allowed us to put thoughts on paper that had been silent until the moment of writing.

David Hunt's work on matched and mismatched classroom teaching and learning environments has remained with me for all my years as a teacher educator. His work has always reminded me to look for the roots of behavior in the interactions between personalities and their shared environments. He and Vygotsky would have had some amazing conversations.

Finally, I appreciate Howard Verman's constant assurance that this work had an audience. His enthusiasm helped keep me going.

x

Introduction

I first began working in multiage classrooms in 1970. Like many other places around the country, Vermont was in the throes of a short-lived infatuation the British primary school model of education. Everywhere in the Green Mountain State, or so it seemed, teachers were opening up their classrooms to let children have more control over what they wanted to learn and how they wanted to learn it. Many teachers embraced the ideas of family grouping, mixed-age classrooms, opening up the physical structures of schools, teaching traditional subjects embedded within thematic, interdisciplinary study, filling their classrooms with interesting things—blocks, sand tables, water play areas, dress up corners, dienes blocks, Cuisenaire rods, pattern blocks, display tables—and teaming with peers to model collaborative learning.

Many teachers did not. Forced by well meaning school administrators to alter their more conventional teaching styles in short periods of time, they resisted the top-down pressure to change and struggled internally as well with the American translation of British practice known as "open education." This reality, combined with a number of other factors, contributed to open education ending almost as quickly as it burst onto the scene.

Vermont had a special history in these years. Buoyed up by a commissioner of education who gave support to "the movement," Vermont schools were encouraged to develop programs that lived up to the Vermont Design for Education, a clarion mission statement for learning that captured the era about as concisely as any statement written in the nation. But, long after the dividers went up in open schools and bookcases began to wall off self-contained graded classrooms and chairs and desks once again faced a room that had a front, some teachers continued to teach in the reformed style and called their settings multiage classrooms.

I have spent a good portion of my professional years in these classrooms, drawn by what seemed to me to be a superior place for children to learn. Children in these settings seemed to be having a good time, to like school, and to be learning. They did interesting things. And their teachers, though working hard and long into the evening, liked their work. It was as if these teachers' relationships with their students somehow served a higher purpose, defined more by "call" than by occupation. Often serving in schools where there was also a "regular way of doing things," they struggled with the professional necessity of not distinguishing between what happened in their rooms and in the "regular" rooms. Often falling back on the rationale that they taught kids who learn in lots of different ways, their reasoning served both to distance themselves from the attributes of the open education movement and to muddle what was truly distinctive about their work. The positive result, however, is that many multiage classrooms remained in Vermont during the 1970s and 1980s. Encouraged by an ever increasing set of developmentally grounded practices, the teachers' work became more grounded and more certain.

I have been privileged to spend time with multiage teachers who in my mind exemplify the best of the lot. They are learners for whom every day is a new day, for whom every moment can be an opportunity to engage a child's mind afresh and a child's heart anew. They are teachers I would describe as believing that learning is as much a spiritual activity as it is an academic exercise. They know from their labors that a child deeply engaged in an investigation that has captured her fascination is engaged in an activity dominated by the mind as well as by the heart. That activity simultaneously defines who she is as a person and the person she will become. This positive affirmation of self has profound consequences. Of course knowledge is constructed. But the by-products of courage, confidence, self-affirmation, and delight are what buttress this most essential core. This is a vision we must hold as we think about what we want for our young children's schooling. This is the start they must have. And regardless of how they come to us, I remain convinced the settings we provide for them must hold this promise.

My own learnings from more than two decades of work in multiage settings can be boiled down to a few statements.

• Multiage teaching refers both to a way of grouping children and a set of teaching practices that work best in such a setting. If neither is present, then the setting isn't an example of multiage teaching, even if children of different grades are grouped together.

• There are many varieties of multiage configurations and no one configuration is best. It all depends on the abilities and likes of the teacher, the professional support she enjoys within the setting, the unique relationship between the school and its local community, and the professional relationships within the school building.

• Continuity is the characteristic that stands out above others in assessing whether or not a setting is multiage in style as well as grouping. Continuity defines multiage and gives it a presence definitively different from a self-contained graded setting that may look very much the same.

• Self-contained graded classroom teachers who share many practices with multiage classroom teachers still have a classroom environment that is different. Gradedness creates issues of "which child is best" and "which child is worst" that result in status differences for children in the classroom organization. Multiage classrooms, because of the mix of ages, have more individualized goals for each child. To fully appreciate this difference, we should try to understand and experience what residence in a class is like as children understand and experience it.

Our beliefs and experience compel us to show interested colleagues how successful multiage settings work, not as recipes for practice, but as a set of portraits. We want to show teachers, teacher educators, and school administrators what our classrooms look like when our practice is successful. Our hope is that the detail, perspective, and decision-making we portray will be illuminating to our colleagues across the country.

In many ways, the profession is in the midst of a paradigm shift from schools as centers of teaching to schools as centers of learning. Multiage practice, as we have written about it, clearly occurs in schools whose focus is on learning. This change has consequences for how we see our roles as teachers, school administrators, and teacher educators. Our present location in the paradigm shift is transitional. This causes discomfort with our various publics to say nothing of the pressures it creates for us as teachers.

Mandating multiage classrooms is an effort to shorten the transition period and create learning-oriented schools. The intent is worthy, but we worry teachers will be placed in complex situations of mixed-age groupings and be expected to perform "magic" without being given time to develop the thought and action that presupposes success in these settings. Teachers need time to change. Perhaps the portraits we share in this book can provide teachers reasons to argue for more appropriate time periods to plan and develop different teaching practices.

We do not pretend to be experts, but we do carry firm beliefs about children as learners and we know what makes our classrooms work. We hope our portraits renew your enthusiasm for teaching in ways that are responsive to children's interests and desires to know more about their world.

Charles Rathbone, Ph.D.
Burlington, Vermont

Part One

The Classroom Study

I undertook the classroom study to understand more about how a multiage classroom works. I chose this particular classroom based on my knowledge of this school and respect for Anne, the teacher. Anne made her choice to participate because of her trust in my openness to learn and my interest in her work. In a sense, The Classroom Study was carried out in this location because two people agreed to bother each other for a while.

I was a participant observer in Anne's room for forty days and her children knew I was approachable for lots of things. Even when I made my notes they knew they could come by and watch. They also knew this was not the time for talk, or at least much talk. I was an involved observer (note 1) (Woods, 1986). Each night I created transcripts of the day's observations although I was rarely exactly up-to-date. Close upon my observations, I began to code and recode my experience as the familiar became more strange. Nevertheless, only when I began to write potential sections of the report did the meaning of what I was seeing really begin to emerge from the pages and pages of information I had generated. It was an intensely personal process.

The Classroom Study addresses four questions that became central to my understanding of this classroom and why things occurred as they did.

1. What a typical day is like in Room A.
2. How this got started: the team.
3. Why these 'typical days' have persisted for so long: the elements of multiage teaching and learning.
4. How Anne is able to do what she does.

One comment with respect to wording. In Vermont, "multiage" refers to the kind of child-responsive practice to be described. In our Vermont context, "mixed-grade" can mean two separate grades in one classroom, each taught separately, not necessarily in concert with what we know about children's learning. Thus, the use of "multiage settings" includes some mixed-grade settings, but not all. We use "Multiage" to refer to Anne's team members and their four classrooms.

Chapter 1

A Day in *Room A*

To satisfy my curiosity about "What is multiage about Multiage?," I spent forty days in this classroom during the winter and spring months of 1990. I watched and wrote about what went on, interviewed and talked with Anne about her work as teacher in this room, and spoke with children about their perceptions of the four classrooms that constitute the Multiage unit. I wrote field notes, took data on children's activity during certain times during the day, interviewed the Multiage teaching team, took a hundred-plus photographs, ate my school lunches in the teachers' room with other staff members, and spent daily life with the children in lots of different and routine ways. They knew me as a writer watching from the sides as well as a person who would zip coats, tie shoelaces, listen to a story, help with double digit subtraction, and ask lots of questions. I did not ride the school bus, follow children or teachers into their homes, interview parents or board members, play with the children on the playground, or spend extensive time in other places in the school. I wanted to find out how one Multiage classroom worked. I wanted to find out how the living and working together of five kindergartners (for half the day), fifteen first, second and third graders, one teacher, and one aide for a day a week affected their learning.

Their daily life in this room as they go through a typical day is what this section is all about, although typical is a misnomer. Each day's schedule is different in rather subtle ways. The day I am describing is a blend of events I came to know as typical. They did not all occur on one day. They just could have. It is one piece of coming to know how they learn, how they get along, how they create their history, and how their history creates them.

The Village School sits just south of the one stop light in a town that has long since become a bedroom community to the state's largest city. Symmetrical and box-like, showing eight large sets of

" I spent forty days in this classroom during the winter and spring months of 1990."

classroom windows to the main street traffic, four from the original building and four from a later addition, the school awaits the buses that bring a majority of its children to its bright red welcoming doors.

8:04 a.m.

"They look like most classes until you notice their heights, the longs and the shorts of them."

On this day the billowing white exhaust from cars of parents pulling into the parking lot belies the fact that the temperature hovers near zero degrees. Most children are bundled in slick, smooth snow gear with slashes of color paintbrushed across their jackets, colors so bright you'd think they must have their own internal battery system. On the whole, the cars pulling in are a tad better off than the cars already parked in the lot, testimony to the fact that this is mostly a community of wealth. The parade of Volvo wagons and Voyager vans are occasionally punctuated by a rusty Plymouth fifteen years old, some family's winter car, put on the road for the salt to eat until spring, whenever it may come. Not all children in Shelburne are well off, just most.

The spinning wheels of cars exiting a bit too quickly indicate that, for many children, school is just one stop in a day of several placements and child care arrangements. The pace is fairly rapid for families in this town.

Today I arrive before the opening bell. Children are allowed into stairwells on either side of the building because of the frigid temperatures. They cluster on the up and down staircases just inside the doors. Noisy groups cling to the stair railings or plop themselves down on the stairs and talk over what's on their minds: last night's sleepover, something they brought to share, the latest tale of the Super Mario Brothers, or what someone said to someone else after school ended yesterday. They politely clear a path for me and through the din I pick my way up the stairs. They know I belong in the school now, they've seen me around and know I'm part of the furniture. The children of Multiage know me as the man who's trying to find out what goes on in their rooms. Just beside the stairs on the wall to my right hangs a fired clay quilt. It is composed of eight rows of ten tiles, shaped and pressed into plant and animal forms by the fingers of a very young boy or girl. "I did one of the squares on that," says Mandy, a third grader of nearly adult sensibilities, as she points to a lumpy pumpkin. "We did it when the third graders were kindergartners. I used clay and my hands." It was unsolicited and said with a measure of pride. I make a mental note to come back to her statement in my log as I round the top of the stairs, move through the double doors, and turn left into Room A. Anne and Phyllis are conversing in the room about last night's school board meeting. An organized group of parents have been giving the teachers continuing concerns as they

4

press their case for roll backs in the budget. Both the budget situation and the contractual agreements are unsettled in the village and district and it provides for a rather dissonant murmur that is constant wherever teachers gather. They are worried and more than a little miffed at what the issues signify concerning the way this part of their public perceives their work. I hang my coat in Anne's closet feeling a bit uncomfortable, like I've entered a private conversation. But I know it isn't. At this level of talk, I am on the inside.

Figure 1

Diagram of Room A

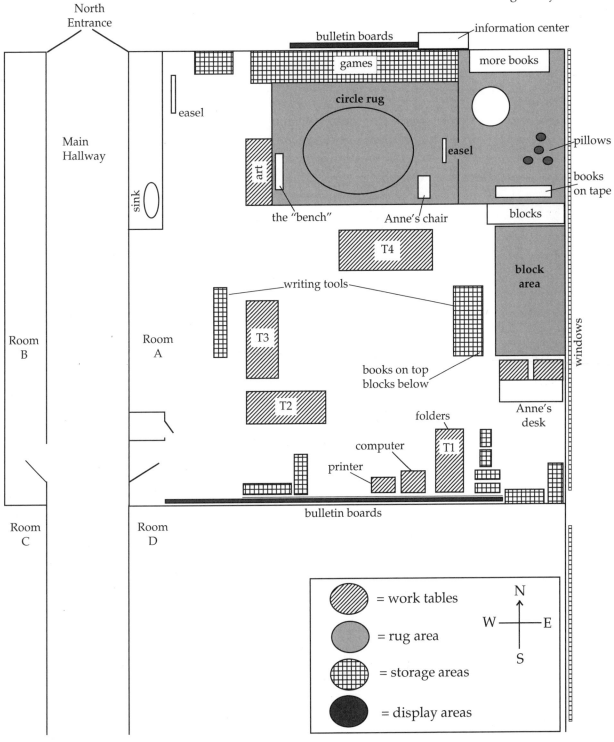

The Gathering:
8:10 a.m.

Morning bell rings, doors swing open, and they file in from the collecting basin at the bottom of the stairs, tumbling, talking, jabbering. Today, it's talk about the fresh snow that fell in a winter that has seen less snow than usual and an unfortunate classmate who slipped and fell in a puddle of cold and sticky mud on the way to his school bus. They look like most classes until you notice their heights, the longs and the shorts of them. This is a group of children unlike a traditionally graded class. They represent three, four, five different ages and five days a week they mostly live together in this large sunny classroom in the northeast corner of this bulging school. They place their boots in the hall, neatly against the wall, then come into the room to hang their coats, mufflers, neck warmers, gloves, and extra sweaters upon the coat hooks. The school day starts almost immediately for all of us and we all show our recognition of that fact in what we do. I gather my notebook and find my seat at the table nearest the circle's edge. Anne has already placed what she needs on the rug next to where she'll be sitting. She arrived almost an hour ago. The children, most of them anyway, in the midst of chatter, joking, and animated conversation, turn their name tags over on the attendance pegboard to signify "I am here!" and find a seat in the gathering circle on the rug. Only those whose week it is on the bench have assigned seats. The rest sit where they will. Five, six, seven, and eight year olds scatter themselves on the rug to begin the day. Our daily routine has already begun.

Multiage consists of four multiage classrooms of twenty children, eighty children in all. Their school day runs from 8:20 in the morning until 2:20 in the afternoon. The kindergartners go home at 11:10 either by bus, parents, or caregivers. With minimal exception, this is the way the Multiage unit has been since 1972. Three of the four multiage teachers started the unit at the beginning. The fourth has been a team member since she moved into the position from a second grade in 1979. The team runs the same daily schedule in each of the four rooms. The rooms are side by side in the main hallway just inside the school from the north door. They have been there since the beginning.

The children are in Multiage by parental request and in Room A by decision of the Multiage team. The children are placed in each of the rooms according to the teachers' notion of balance. Balance is achieved by grouping kids with a proper mix of ages, learning styles, ability levels, gender, classroom behavior, and the number of years in the same room. They try to achieve balance in academic skills, social behaviors, interests, curiosity, and activity level. The team has a rule of thumb: no more than two consecutive years with any one teacher unless there is good reason to do otherwise. They judge there to be enough similarity across the four rooms that the children ought to experience getting along with more than one teacher during their tenure in the unit. The rooms are intentionally similar though not congruent in physical arrangement, daily schedule, and rules of conduct. Across the four rooms, teacher expectations are similar. From time to time, children from other rooms spend time in Room A while their teacher is on a field trip. I never observed confusion about what was expected of them.

Opening Circle:
8:25 a.m.

Opening circle is never announced or heralded. It merely begins. The children know the routine. You come in the room, put your things away, talk casually with friends, flip your attendance card and "come to circle." Susie, a second grader, tells me exactly what she has to do.

"Well, I have to turn over my name, and then I have to get my shoes on, and I have to take my lunch out of my backpack, and put it over there in the coatroom. And if you were attendance, well, you'd go over there and write down (how many were absent). Then she (the teacher) tells us what we're going to do in the day, and she tells us how to get the lunch count, and then we do like a special activity, and then we have classes like art or music or gym, whatever, and then we come back."

Opening circle begins the day, a time to gather together and start. Routines of attendance, calendar, menu, and sharing are accomplished. With menu, there is always a problem to solve.

Jimmy does the lunch count. There are nine turkey sandwiches, one ham and cheese, and five milks.

Anne's question is, "How many more children are having a hot lunch than milk?"

When Jimmy, a first grader, frowns, she gives him a hint.

"This is a two-step problem. What are the steps? I'm not looking for the answer, just the steps."

In Room A, there are always things to learn and even the most natural situation, like ordering today's lunch, can provide the setting. In fact, the more normal the setting, the more natural the question.

Once the routines of attendance, calendar, and lunch count are over, selected children have a time to share. They may share one thing that has happened to them. The group is always a mixed-age group, and it is always the same group that sits on "the bench." The bench is a storage box at one end of the circle that children like to sit upon. It is one of those places of seemingly magical attraction to young children. To solve the problem of too many children always

"They try to achieve balance in academic skills, social behaviors, interests, curiosity, and activity level."

wanting to sit there, the class made a rule that the children who were scheduled to share on any given day would be the children who also were allowed to sit on the bench. The sharing schedule was posted on the easel right next to the teacher. Everyone could see it, every-one knew, and those who cared to look knew who was to share each day of the week. For Anne, sharing was an important part of the daily routine. But more than routine, it was important because of the personal connections made among the children during this time. Sharing also helps to anchor each child in the day. Anne sees this time in a way that characteristically both appreciates the diversity and uses the diversity inherent in what the children share because of their age span.

"When I give kids an opportunity to share, the younger kids bring something, often just a toy. I discourage that as they get older. I really encourage them to be telling something like a piece of news. The younger have to hold on to something sometimes to feel com-fortable. Now, I think the sharing is worth taking time for because it gives them the chance to tell their own story which begins to build a feeling by them and by others of 'who I am.'"

8:33 a.m.

On this particular day, it is time for Lindy, Betsy, Laurie, and Adam to share. Sally interrupts to share something with us "real quickly." Anne and the class permit this because they know Sally as a child who needs constructive and positive time with them.

"The puppies have diarrhea. Yesterday they ate a bottle of vitamins."

She smiles and laughs and the group smiles along with her. Anne goes on. She asks Lindy if she has anything? Lindy shakes her head, "No."

Betsy shows us an old horseshoe that she found with her father while walking around the farm. "It was sticking half way out of the ground!"

Anne reflects, "How did you ever find it? You must have very good eyes." Betsy talks some more about the walk with her Dad.

Laurie's turn now. She says, "I think it's too late but can I go get something from my jacket pocket? It's in a plastic bag."

Anne replies, "I think not, Laurie. You remember to bring them in at the beginning of share time."

Someone else notes "Laurie always waits until it's late!"

"Adam has brought something in he's made at home."

Adam brings three cardboard box constructions to circle. They are decorated with a variety of objects: pads of paper, plastic keys, an electronic baseball game, and a small graduation hat. The largest construction travels into circle on its own accord. It is mounted on a battery operated car. Adam has made a traveling robot. Another of the three he calls "The Cage." In it are three constructed hamsters,

Lego-like, complete with food. Adam said he wanted to get one because his dog had recently died. Construction number two is the traveling robot. Adam explains.

"This guy was the best. I made it. It took the longest. The box is mounted on a car. Back here is where I can put stuff. It just graduated from college. It wears its notes on the side."

Anne asks, "Now what are those other things on the side? I said we brought in peaceful things."

Adam replies, "They're missiles but they're defensive. They just stop things."

He goes on and talks about the hamsters. He has brought in a tape recorder and has recorded a message to the class from the hamsters.

"I am seven times e3. I am programmed to help people. I am x72. We are Twinkle, Gaze, and Speedy. We all run track."

All this is too much for Ethan. He flings around his loose sleeves and makes mega-explosions in the air.

Anne notices but doesn't draw attention to him. "Let's put all these back in the corner for now and they can come out at Explore Time. Well, that was quite a share. How many of you have used cardboard boxes to make things?"

A typical sharing time in Room A. Real pieces of real lives. Living present and accounted for. Pets born and died, pennies fused in a frightening barn fire, a walk through a meadow with a father recently separated from his daughter, a shoebox creation painstakingly figured out and glued together at home, all shared in a matter-of-fact manner. The children listen and mostly pay careful attention. The rules governing the interaction were set long before. They lie just under the surface now. Rules maintained in part by the children who have been in Room A for more than this year.

> **Rule One.** You can pass if you want to.
> **Rule Two.** You can't leave the circle to get something once sharing has begun.
> **Rule Three.** You cannot interrupt someone else's sharing.
> **Rule Four.** Keep the sharing as short as you can because some of us can't sit still for long periods of time.
> **Rule Five.** Items shared may be left out for others to investigate during Explore Time with your permission.
> **Rule Six.** Sally can interrupt as long as her sharing is quick because we've agreed this is important for Sally.

"A typical sharing time in Room A. Real pieces of real lives."

Sharing time is a way of gathering in pieces of the children's lives, giving those pieces a place in the presence that is the classroom, starting the day with a decidedly human tone, and sometimes suggesting activities the children might pursue at school or at home from an idea shared by one of the children. Sharing time honors the lives of the children by letting each child know what is going on in their classmates' lives. It is a time from which curriculum can evolve, and it makes ideas present for all to hear that may later turn into projects or at the very least, conversations.

Theme Time:
9:02 a.m.

Anne now takes back the direction of the opening circle. She shifts the purpose of the circle from sharing to more directed action—action directed by her. Theme time follows. During theme time children work on writing projects or activities related to a specific theme they are studying. During this time of my residence, the theme under study was a science/social studies theme on nutrition and foods. Earlier in the day, I noticed aesthetically arranged collections of fruit on three tables in the room as well as on the easel shelf next to Anne's place at circle. The children had recently been studying fruit as part of this unit and Anne has planned for the children to do some sketching of the still lifes as part of their thematic study. Anne settles down the conversation that bubbled after Adam's robot departed the circle. The routine shifts.

"Whoa. I had something planned and I thought we might squeeze it in partly today and partly tomorrow. I put out the 'Hello Health Foods' folders. I have created still lifes on the tables. We have these pictures from the library and I asked Mrs. Senflieber (the art teacher) to find me some more. Now we've had pictures that we've looked at and sketched."

Jamie and Ethan are fooling around with the fruit in one of the arrangements. Anne reprimands them sharply: "Now put the food back! I've arranged it kind of carefully!"

She goes on once again in her typically gentle voice. The difference in tone is not subtle and everyone catches her message.

"Now we've had pictures that we've looked at and sketched. You can choose to draw a little arrangement. You can do one from a print or sit on the rug with a board and draw this arrangement (on the easel table). You can copy just part of it. I have a couple of books out on the table over there. Someone might want to use this. It has beautiful pictures of all kinds of fruits. "

Someone spontaneously bursts forth, "Look at the letters!"

Anne continues. "And I have this book with an arrangement on the title page. Isn't it beautiful? I got out the new plastic crayons. Let's not use markers. The crayons are a bit softer. Look at the shapes real closely. Tomorrow I'll show you a paper I have about straight and curved lines."

The children are making their choices, They go to a place in the room where they want to work. "I'm coming around with paper."

I listen to the talk in one of the collected groups drawing the vase on the semicircular table.

> "Frank, look what I did!"
> "Oh yeah. That's really good."
> "It's perfect."
> "How'm I going to draw the vase?"
> "Mrs. B., look at how close I came to that green-blue!"

The children are really involved. It's as if there is a hunger for this kind of activity for all of them right now.

Theme time is an ongoing continuation of more than a month's work studying foods and food-related health issues. Today's particular action is also an important activity in its own right. The drawing. The focused observation. On this particular day it is intense. I note in my log the ages of the children sitting together in the four groups. Two of the tables are self-selected mixed-age groupings and two of the tables are self-selected same-age groupings. The mixed-aged groupings are adjacent ages, not five year olds and seven year olds, or six year olds and nine year olds. I note, "There is some multiage here but multiage is not the point. The point is involvement and intensity and safety in trying new things with 'friends.'" The children choose both their arrangement of fruit and their arrangement of drawing companions. Perhaps it is safer to sit with first-grade friends or second-grade friends, or second- and third-grade friends. The mixed-ages in this activity are of maximum spread.

As quickly as it begins, a quiet and public realization by Anne draws the time to a close.

"Oh my. I have to make an announcement about stopping. We must figure out how to keep these works safe. It's time to pick up. Put your name on the back and pile them on the table."

Theme time has taken seventeen minutes today. It's now time for specials.

Specials:

Art, music, library, and gym constitute the specials. In the whole history of the Multiage program, the specialist teachers have never agreed to teach mixed-age groupings. Every week, at whatever arbitrary time is finally arrived at in the master schedule, work abruptly stops in multiage and the children, grouped by age across the four multiage classrooms, go off to their specials. The consequence of this event relates to the issue of time. Time is a fluid quantity in multiage. The teachers want time to be variable for two reasons: 1) if the children are deeply engaged in their work, as they

"The point is involvement and intensity and safety in trying new things with 'friends.'"

were in Anne's room during the still life painting, the time period can blend into the next scheduled event; and 2) if time is the variable, then learning becomes more of a constant. The effect of having to section the children off by grade level for specials is to create an absolute blocking point during the day. This arbitrary segmentation places an "outside limitation" on children's time for engaged and sustained work. On this day, the third graders go to library, the second graders to art, the first graders to music, and the kindergartners to gym. The children line up in Room A according to grade level groupings and one by one each group is called to the hallway to join its same-age cohort from the other rooms. They are sent on their way by any or all of the Multiage team.

This now begins one of the few times during the day members of the team see each other. In the forty minutes that follow, they meet as a team or use the time individually for class preparation. Most often, I saw the time being used for preparation although this may have been a factor for Anne and me only. It was one of the few blocks of time that informal talk could occur. Anne and I would sit and talk for twenty minutes or so, then Anne would start to provision the room for Explore Time. I'd help where I could. Provisioning was making sure snack food was ready for either preparation or eating, the desks were clean, materials were ready for her Explore Time group (if she was to have one), and the various tools (paper, pencils, markers, crayons, blocks) were ready to go.

Explore Time:
10:10 a.m.

Explore Time begins with the children returning from their specials. They pick up their snack (today it is a bagel and cream cheese prepared by the kindergartners) and get right to "work" (their word, not mine). Explore Time will continue until around 10:55 when Anne will gently turn off the lights and say something inclusive and simple. "We need to pick up and get our books out." This statement will signal the beginning of pick-up and the end of Explore Time. By 11:00 a.m., all but a few children will be doing their silent reading and the room will be quiet. In the fifty intervening minutes, children will be engaged in the most complex of social interactions, prodded occasionally by Anne, but mostly determined, selected, begun, and ended on their own. (note 2)

On this particular day, between 10:10 and 11:00 a.m., thirty-five children participated in the explore activities in Anne's room. The room is busy, but not the least bit frenetic. The four rooms of Multiage schedule Explore Time simultaneously and children are free to navigate from room to room. During this Explore Time, I watch the children select and pursue the following activities:

1. Two younger girls look through a classroom picture album

that contains autobiographies written by the children of Room A alongside a picture of each child.

2. Three of the four older children use Legos and imagination to construct a space station. They talk constantly about their construction and all matter of things.

3. Nine children representing all classroom ages build parallel and series circuits with batteries and bulbs.

4. Several children alone and together measure a variety of "edges" in the room that (1) identifies the edge that matches a string length posted in opening circle and (2) answers a riddle about that edge.

5. Three older boys work at the computer playing with a program that presents the children with a series of problems about momentum, friction, and weight.

6. Several children over the course of Explore Time listen to taped stories while following along with the actual book.

7. One older boy builds imaginary animals from pipe cleaners and cotton balls.

8. Three older girls practice double-digit addition problems in math using worksheets, Unifix cubes, and each other.

9. Two younger boys build a marble maze from a set of blocks designed for that purpose.

10. A group of boys use the large, wooden construction blocks to construct an elaborate ramp structure that turns out to be a garage/landing platform for all kinds of wheeled and flying objects.

11. A series of children play Battleship.

12. Several children, mostly boys of several ages, work with Multiplex Cubes and little rubber bears. They build all kinds of flying vehicles of constantly changing shape.

13. A second- and a third-grade girl painstakingly complete a self-designed worksheet on the beginning letters of the last name of all eighty children in multiage.

14. Two younger boys build a garage for their cars with smaller construction blocks.

This morning, Anne joins the work at the batteries and bulbs table. Her presence is another way of "salting the works." The batteries and bulbs were introduced the week before as a result of interest shown during a Friday morning special in the late autumn. (note 3) The activity lasts the full forty minutes of Explore Time. As Explore Time opened, two second-grade boys and one first-grade boy were involved with the activity. Soon after they were joined by one third-grade girl. Over the course of the activity, others joined in. In total, nine children worked with Anne and the bulbs this morning.

Activity that persisted for the full time or for most of it included work at the computer, the listening center, Lego construction, pipe cleaner construction, and the math work. The measuring activity

"The children take time to stop by the work of their friends, watch, sometimes cheer, and often comment."

was tried by first, second, and third graders working together, talking about their hunches and false alarms. There was at least one "floater," (note 4) but at no time did the number of floaters exceed three and no floaters persisted for more than five minutes.

Ethan and Jamie build with smaller blocks. They work out how to construct a garage to hold their small trucks. Both boys are highly involved youngsters and each likes to hold his ground. Play between them is always intense, sometimes contentious, and always loyal. During this time, Jamie backed one of his trucks into some of the blocks Ethan was using to build and knocked them over. Tears welled in Ethan's eyes and he said with sharp frustration, "The blocks were not just working!" Jamie looked away as if he were looking for the person who had knocked the blocks astray, turned back and said he was sorry, that he didn't mean to do it. The two managed to work out their difficulty and remained builders for the rest of Explore Time. They were smiling again within fifteen seconds of Ethan's outburst. The modeling of problem solving at various times across the year in Room A has contributed to their resolution of the conflict of the moment.

The questions Anne raises at the batteries and bulbs table softly permeate the air space in the room. She suggests avenues of exploration.

"Can you light two bulbs?"

"Does it make any difference how you put the wire on the battery?"

"What happens if you turn the battery around?"

Older children had started to work with the materials recreating some of the circuits they had built in past encounters. Her questions propel the exploration. It has been at least three months since any child had "played" with these particular materials in Room A, although clearly there is memory of connections that worked previously. A child tells me another Multiage room has had the batteries and bulbs available for play fairly recently. Anne has her clipboard and is recording what children say and do for future reference. Perhaps one child's work here will reappear in a story written later in the day or as a familiar setting for a math problem later that afternoon. She is working with three girls at this point, and they are trying to build parallel circuits.

"Why do you suppose that might have happened?" she asks.

At another table the computer software encourages cooperative participation. At least that is the way Anne has taught these children to use it. The sharing and helping atmosphere pervading Explore Time provides a healthy context for computer games so its purpose is exploration, not competition. This game might have been very competitive in a different classroom. In here, a setting that is materials rich, a setting where children have to learn from each other, the children work together with the computer activity. Anne sees this work as valuable.

14

10:35 a.m.

Nine self-selected activities are being pursued in Room A and eight children from other Multiage rooms participate. The room is a busy hum. Anne knows her noise tolerance is higher than that of her team-mates. She attributes this to her early childhood background. She prefers having large motor activities in her room because she likes watching what the children will make of them, although there are some days she wonders why. Today is not one of those days. Today the children are quite business-like about their work. There are plenty of smiles going around, especially when a "win" occurs at the computer, a new circuit is achieved for the first time, or when another module of the space station is completed. The children take time to stop by the work of their friends, watch, sometimes cheer, and often comment. The commentary rarely seems to diminish the activity. It is usually brief, then it's back to business as usual.

The conversations in Explore Time are intricate. Dyson (1990) writes of the multi-layered nature of children's conversations. Her observations were certainly my experience in this classroom. The following conversation between Jerry and Ryan, two kindergartners, is illustrative. It is Explore Time on a Monday morning just after Monday morning journals. (note 5) The children are drawing posters for an upcoming play and are recalling a time during the past week-end when Ryan played at Jerry's house. Jerry's family had just moved into a new house and during sharing time, Jerry has been treating everyone to seemingly endless stories about the move. During their discussion in the midst of drawing and sharing ideas and poster creations, a moment occurred where Ryan said something Jerry didn't hear. Jerry thinks he should have.

Jerry: "What did you say?"

Ryan: "You say?"

Jerry: "You."

Ryan: "I didn't say anything!"

Jerry: "You just said" (and he stands up beside his desk, looks at Ryan and mouths some words, lips barely moving, no sound coming out).

They laugh together although Jerry seems a bit uncomfortable. Perhaps it is me watching although I'm trying to remain casually involved in my note taking.

Ryan: "No, I wasn't."

Jerry: "Oh, I was watching my dad. And wasn't it funny when I helped him bring in the rug?"

Ryan: "Yehhh."

Jerry: "You should have shot me when I was doing on the drum "bing, bom, bamm" (he pretends to hit a drum).

They laugh and go back to drawing. They draw silently for about two seconds.

> *"For the most part, children are deeply absorbed in their work."*

Ryan: "Do you still think this is dumb? (He points to his picture by hitting it with his pencil tip.)"

Jerry: "No."

Ryan: " 'Cause I still could make this (pointing to another part on the picture), use this eraser on this."

Jerry: "I need some yellow."

And they draw some more, eyes very focused on their pictures, without comment.

In these moments are friendship, the modeling of pictures, the processing of a weekend, casual conversation, a direct request for feedback and a direct answer to the request, an expressed need for some more yellow, and spending time with a friend in meaningful activity. And this is just one of a multitude of such events in a fifty-minute period of time.

Control in Explore Time is subtle. Anne's occasional disallowing of an activity or an action not withstanding, Explore Time has existed for all these years because the activity that occurs is intimately connected to the real interests and life knowledge of the children. For the most part, children are deeply absorbed in their work. The number of floaters is minimal or nonexistent. The children remain engaged with their materials, with each other, regardless of age. If something doesn't work or if they finish their work with a material, it is returned to its place, the child walks away and chooses something else to do. Their talk about life events is concurrent with the activities they pursue. The purpose of the activity varies and it appears the children are not all that aware of or even care about the functionality of the activities beyond the immediate moment. I see them practicing work that will be needed later in the day or week. I see them extending things they do to new situations. I see exercise of their imaginations where the process of their activity is more important than its final outcome. I see cooperative problem solving occasioned by situations that arise as a direct result of their play. But what I see and conclude about my observations of what they do and what their intentions might be probably hold quite different meanings. Each has its own validity.

In the midst of it all, I see the constant watching and listening to what's going on around them, an action I call "sitting in" on other children's activities. The metaphor of a jazz musician sitting in seems apt for what I observe. Just as sitting in with an admired ensemble enables a musician to learn new phrasings, fingerings, and melodic lines, the children in Multiage seem to cause a similar kind of learning as they sit in on other children's activity. They eavesdrop on the action, they watch it, they may replicate it, they adjust it to their own interests, and they learn it in their own unique manner. For new initiates to an activity, sitting in allows them to anticipate their own eventual performance. They can reject it for the time being or sometimes even forever. For example, conversation surrounding the batteries and bulbs meant everyone in Anne's classroom could know something about the batteries and bulbs even though only nine children participated directly in the activity. This didn't happen by chance. Anne planned its occurrence in this seemingly casual and informal manner. The structure of Explore Time is high, though subtle.

The environment created during Explore Time is an extremely fertile one for learning about all kinds of things in all kinds of ways. Each child proceeds at his or her own chosen pace and level. And Anne watches it all. In her watching, the activities of days to come get shaped and adjusted according to what she learns by her observations of the children who participate. She learns of their interests, their capacities, their weaknesses, their styles of engaging the world around them. Explore Time is a time of intensity that creates a high level of focused, purposeful engagement on the part of children. The interest creates a kind of momentum all its own, a momentum that spills over into other parts of the day and creates the overall tone to multiage that is particularly representative of this classroom.

10:53 a.m.

"Okay. We've got a lot of work to clean up." This sentence, spoken quietly, announced by a flick of the light switch, accomplishes two ends: it announces the completion of Explore Time and it directs the transition to silent reading. I was continually in awe of how quickly and orderly Explore Time ended and how the beginning of the end was always signaled with such gentle inclusiveness. I would observe the same ritual again at the end of silent reading.

The children begin to put their things away. Legos go back to the shelf, the unfinished space station is carefully placed on top of the block case for safe keeping, the batteries and bulbs are disassembled and placed in several baskets put back in their proper place. Pens, markers, crayons, pencils—all are returned to their shelves. Scrap papers are picked up from around the tables and thrown in the recycling bin, the computer is shut down and covered. Children go to their cubbies or choose a book from numerous containers of similarly difficult reading material in several locations in the room. Occasionally Anne directs someone to a specific task. Most of the time, the children follow the clean-up routine set earlier in the year. Specific tasks are tagged for specific children on the job chart. The kindergartners get ready to depart to baby-sitters, day care, or for some, home. Quite independently they tug on their winter clothes. They leave by 11:00 a.m. In six minutes it is done.

Silent Reading Time:
11:00 a.m.

Some children sit at tables, others on the rug in the circle area,

"It is a reading program based in real literature that intertwines intimately with a process method for writing."

one under the easel for privacy. Unlike most days when the murmurs of children vocalizing to themselves can be heard, the room is still today. Anne positions herself on a chair in front of the room near the front table. She calls Ethan to sit and read with her. Jamie will follow. During the next twenty minutes the children will be engaged with print at mostly self-selected levels. The younger children usually read picture books or their own journal writing. The older children's reading ranges from beginning readers to complex chapter books. All matter of reading material except one is in sight for all the children. No basal readers are present. These literature books are chosen independently from containers in the room or from the library. The room is still. Mixed-age groupings sit at self-selected seats. Everyone reads. If someone needs help, a neighbor or friend is asked, hence the murmurs. Anne listens intently to Ethan and assesses his progress while he reads with her. She writes occasional notes to herself. It is a reading program based in real literature that intertwines intimately with a process method for writing. Reading and writing are of the same fabric. The children read and write throughout the day and in the afternoon they are often read to. This is one time when everyone reads quietly together. It is as focused as Explore Time but in quite a different way.

"I guess we'd better find a stopping place." It's over. The snap of shutting books signals the end of silent reading and the anticipation of food and exercise.

Lunch and Outdoor Recess:

We all line up and have a brisk walk to the gym where hot lunch is served. Today, it's porcupine burgers and yellow pudding. After lunch the children return to the room briefly to get ready for outside recess. Anne eats rapidly in the teachers' room for she has to be back to Room A when the children return to dress for recess. During recess time she will prepare the room for the afternoon, make a phone call, meet with the special educator and school social worker about a child of concern, and have a cup of tea.

Afternoons in Anne's room are a "work" time in the more conventional sense of the word. Each child owns two folders—a math folder and a language arts folder. On Monday mornings before school begins, Anne places a contract in each folder specifying a "chunk" of work to be done in each subject area. It is each child's responsibility to complete the assigned work over the course of the week. Often worksheets accompany the contracts or pages of work in other books are specified in the contract. Various forms of writing are required depending upon what the child happens to be studying at the time. Unlike the morning, more of the afternoon work represents conventional graded work and the children seem to know who is doing what. Some have similar assignments. Some have different assignments. Like the morning, they are free to help each other when needed although the preferred mode of learning is individualized work pursued independently. Because the room is arranged with tables, children of different ages inevitably sit next to each other and as in all the other times in Multiage, they naturally seek help from those who know about what they are trying to learn more about. Math work will see more like-aged children helping each other. More cross-age help occurs in the language arts.

Most afternoons have four distinct time blocks. A short circle time usually begins the afternoon. The children gather after recess, settle down and settle in, and orient themselves to the affairs of the afternoon. Anne often reads a chapter book to the children during this time. She may also use this time to introduce an activity germane to folder activities. For example, all children might be developing a story about a friend. Anne would use the time to demonstrate the creation of a story web, a useful skill for any child working on a writing assignment.

Circle time usually ends the day as well. The final circle time creates a space for children to talk about and show something they learned during the day and quite possibly to think about work they will engage in the following day. Individual children may share specific pieces of writing or mathematical discoveries they have made during the afternoon.

In between the afternoon circles is time for math and language arts. These two time blocks run thirty to forty minutes and alternate in sequence every other week. This blocking permits the flexibility to allow time to run over into the next block should the children need more time in their opening circle or the first time block. Early in the year, the class realized the first time block consistently impinged upon the second time block. The problem was brought to circle and the children decided to alternate the order of work times so they wouldn't be consistently shortchanged on the second time block. Because specials occur in the morning, afternoon times are relatively unencumbered.

The afternoon provides flexibility for grouping. There are times when the Multiage teachers share children so one teacher can work with all first graders (for example) to carry out a specific piece of directed instruction. Or, a given teacher might arrange to have just her own first graders for a similar purpose.

It is also possible to use the afternoon time block to carry out special projects. In late April, Anne and her children created a set of one-act plays about Winnie the Pooh. Rehearsals proceeded for three weeks and they eventually consumed all the afternoon time. Indeed, during the last week of the play, activity time and Explore Time were devoted to various aspects of the production as well.

The power of time flexibility cannot be overestimated. The

"The power of time flexibility cannot be overestimated."

opportunity to group and regroup permits Anne to focus direct instruction on children who need it, thereby varying the function of time to enable more learning to occur. Because different groupings continually and naturally occur in Multiage, these specific skill-focused groupings do not seem unusual to the children. No particular group gets labeled pejoratively because they happen to be spending extra time with the teacher on a regular, patterned basis. Every child at one point or another spends extra time with the teacher alone or with many different combinations of children. The variance of time and the invariance of learning is one keynote of this mixed-age setting.

Opening Afternoon Circle:
12:20 p.m.

The children clamber back into the room from recess. It is the time of year when mud clumps seem to take root and grow on the floor. Though he is oblivious to it, Ethan's boots are both collectors and depositors of huge mud clumps. Anne prods, "Wouldn't you be more comfortable in sneakers, Ethan, now that winter is pretty much over?" The next day Ethan leaves his boots in the hall. The day after he brings sneakers. The room is noticeably quieter without the clomping of his boots. It is noticeably cleaner as well.

The children gather in circle excited about events during recess. Some are settling down, others are not. The chill of the morning has been replaced by warmer sunshine. Given the frigid early morning, the afternoon seems positively hot. Anne begins to talk but too many of the children keep their own conversations going. She looks around for a moment, then claps her hands sharply: "Let's change what we are talking about, now!" She leans forward and makes circular motions with both hands, as if she is pulling them to the center of the circle, pulling them to attention. They get the not-too-subtle hint and quiet down. She goes over the contracts in their folders, reviews how many days are left in the week and asks the children to figure out what they must do before the week ends. She displays yesterday's work on brainstorming story ideas and asks the children how their own brainstorming went. They are attentive to her but their responses indicate too many of them don't quite get the idea of what they are to do. Adam and Ray are talking too much to each other about things other than the subject at hand. She separates them and says, "You two need to pay more attention." Her tone is matter of fact. The act of separating is done with hand motions. The two readily move apart to other locations in the circle. Anne returns to her teaching and asks Laurie if she can use her brainstorm as an example of what she wants them to learn to do. Laurie explains what she did in exacting detail. A wave of head nods and, "Oh, I see!" show the younger children have begun to catch on. Anne ends this short lesson by having the children talk about "audience" and what details they think would interest their chosen audience. She then uses her own story ideas as a model to illustrate interest, recency, and story power. She has previously told the class three different ideas she has for a story. One idea is about a young squirrel she saw running down a phone wire. Another idea concerns some of the children in the class and how they go about their learning. She wants them to tell her which of her stories they would choose on the basis of its interest for them.

> Anne: "Now, do you have some ideas?"
> Jamie: "How about when the squirrel learned to tightrope walk?"
> Anne: "That's a good one. Now when you know enough, when you have enough ideas, think what other things your audience would like to read about. Then write it. I'm thinking of publishing your story in book form again."
> Adam: "Like last year?"

Anne participates in the process. Despite the apparent interest in the squirrel story, she decides to write about "school stories." She has been asked to deliver a presentation on multiage teaching at a teachers' conference in New Hampshire and she is using this time to write about her classroom. It is a nice example of her modeling real events, something she is asking of her students. What she asks of the children, she will do herself. And she will share one of her stories just as she asks them to share their writing. Anne too is one of the writers in Room A.

Language Arts and Math Time:
12:50 p.m.

The children break from circle and get their math folders. This is a "math first" week. They sit where they wish and start in on their contract work. Anne calls two children to join her on the rug. They bring their folders, she gets some colored trading chips, and proceeds to work them through a sequence of borrowing and trading. She is concerned about their acquisition of the place value concept and is trying to identify where gaps in their knowledge lie. She's wondering if it is a factual omission or if their inabilities lie more in a lack of procedural knowledge. She works with them for perhaps twenty minutes, shifting back and forth between collections of ten objects and the numerals that represent those collections. She starts with simple identifications and works into borrowing and carrying double-digit numbers. It's hard work and the children stick with it. The noise level in the room rises as she focuses her efforts on Frank and Betsy.

Having children work independently presents its own special complexities. The children move at their own pace, and groupings

"A wave of head nods and, 'Oh, I see!' show the younger children have begun to catch on."

based on shared concept and skill acquisition constantly reform. It is an ongoing challenge to balance the responsibility of knowing what they need with her ability to deliver instruction in the way she knows it needs to be done. The frustration of this constant balancing act is apparent in a comment she makes to me.

"Frank needs division. I'm putting him off until Mandy is ready for it. A group is ready for borrowing, these children here (pointing) are ready for multiplication, and these guys here are ready to start regrouping. Suddenly in the last week I've got all these groups ready to go on to something new and I can't possibly do it all at once. You have to give them kind of a tutorial period, then practice, and then they are off on their own. These new groups all need tutorials now."

At any one time during the math block, children are working on reinforcing knowledge just acquired, practicing concepts in the process of formation, consolidating knowledge by using new applications of the recently acquired concept, or waiting for a new group to form. It is tedious work for most children and seemingly less motivating than their morning activities. They are more distracted in the afternoon and their folders seem to take the brunt of their resistance to task. As they work at their desks, the work folders become the place where equations are worked out, additions are practiced, and doodling occurs while the brain is thinking things through. Their pace slows down but they seem to get their quota done every week and they do progress. And every day, some children get very directed instruction that is delivered in a manner that seems to maximize their chances of learning what they need to learn. During all the math blocks I observed, I always saw children working with manipulatives and drawings that stood for concepts as well as the more abstract numerical representations of concepts. Any concept under construction was practiced minimally in these three modes, usually starting at the concrete level and moving through the more abstract numerical representations. Often, the modes overlapped.

At 1:30, Anne asks the children "to finish the section you're working on and put away your math folder." They do, some quite rapidly. They find their language arts folders and move to a seat to begin that work. For the next half-hour the children work away on writing work. Jamie practices writing a story about a worm in a little booklet Anne has made for him. It is laborious work but he sticks to it. The necessity for fine motor control creates a situation that is very different from his morning play with cars and trucks. Yet I wonder if his morning success helps fuel his determination this afternoon on a task that has been chosen for him. Ethan practices cursive letters. He does five in a twenty minute period, talking to Jamie all the while. Jamie finally moves away from his chatter. Sally

22

tries to get Susie to draw a butterfly for her and Mandy is working quietly on her brainstorm. The rest of the class seems to be in the idea-generating stage of story writing and many use the brainstorming technique Anne demonstrated during opening circle. The chatter level is quite noticeable in the room but Anne does not attend to it. She is working intently with Betsy on her story reading. Another maze to find her way through. She is concerned about Betsy's reading and feels she should be moving ahead more smoothly. Betsy isn't, and Anne wants to know why.

Closing Circle:

At 2:00 p.m., Anne says quietly, "I think we should find a stopping place and do some story sharing." Again, the inclusive, quiet request. Energy erupts and fills the transition. When the children gather on the rug Anne has them take three deep breaths and settle themselves onto the rug. She answers Sally's question and moves Ray. She sets up the author's chair and Frank volunteers to read his story. The children mostly listen. It is filled with Nintendo imagery, and the children attend quietly as he draws to a close yet another tale of the Super Mario Brothers. Ethan is next. They listen silently. Laurie follows. Then Anne, who uses the occasion to review the rules and purpose for author's chair. Her story is about two girls giving each other positive and negative feedback. There is lots of emotion written into it and the drama captures the children. She makes the distinction for them between feedback that pushes too hard and feedback that is helpful.

Then it is time to go. The children stretch away from the circle, gather their coats and line up to meet the school buses. Several girls remain in the room. Mandy has Girl Scouts (they meet in the gym), and Becky is being picked up by another mother who today arrives five minutes late. Usually she's ten minutes early. It has been an afternoon where the children's energy has wanted to burst like the spring weather outside. Anne has used up a good deal of hers keeping them focused.

It is 2:20 p.m. and the school day ends.

"It has been an afternoon where the children's energy has wanted to burst like the spring weather outside."

23

Chapter 2

The Larger Context: The Multiage Team

Multiage started in 1972 as part of the Alternative Staffing Project, a federally funded local community education development program to organize alternative schooling programs for children in two schools. Influential townspeople formed the initial steering group to seek funding. Their interest was not so much because conditions in the school were bad, it was more in keeping with the times. Vermont's State Board of Education (1968) had recently published "The Vermont Design for Education," a statement of progressive schooling principles modeled after the tenets of Britain's Infant Schools. Featherstone (1971), Silberman (1973), Rogers (1970), and others were writing about a more informal, child-centered kind of schooling than was conventionally practiced in the United States. The advocacy of new approaches was occurring partly to change the conditions of schooling in an urban America that was increasingly unwilling to put up with educational practices that systematically eliminated most children of poverty from the promises of success that had customarily accompanied "hard work" in school (Fantini and Weinstein, 1968). The team interview shows a similar inclination to address the fundamental issue of educational equality regardless of social class in the Alternative Staffing Project. It was clear that "schools should be doing that."

"One of the issues, in order to get any money, was that the program had to be a joint venture between two different schools of two different towns . . . and so it was unique that Charlotte and Shelburne agreed to do this. . . . Charlotte was very rural at that point. . . and they really wanted a cross-section of children as part of the pupils, . . . a cross-section of economic background and just all different types of children. . . ."

Marion Stroud was hired to direct the project. She was influential in the formation of The Prospect School in Bennington, Vt., a school known for its child-centered educational practice. She created a three-year development plan for the project. The first year was a planning year, the program was implemented in the second year, and the third year was for consolidation. Teachers were selected and trained in the first year and the training included four days of observation and participation at The Prospect School. They visited other classrooms representative of the British model, they read, they planned, they selected materials, they participated in numerous community meetings. The second year they began teaching. During this year the primary grade unit for the program was housed at the Charlotte school and the Shelburne children were bused daily to Charlotte after they arrived at Shelburne. Dissatisfaction with this aspect of the program was quite strong so the third year of the program saw the primary grade unit split into two groups—the Shelburne team and the Charlotte team. In 1990, three of the four original members of the Shelburne team still taught in Multiage.

This part of the history is important for several reasons. The program was not imposed on the community. It came about because of an influential community group's "ground swell" of interest in the educational program of the British Infant Schools.

"We were in the throes of a lot of different kinds of classes, homogeneous classes, so (the project) was a break away from that (form of education. We had) a feeling that this was good education for most everyone which is something we've always maintained."

It came about because of a sense that the teachers and staff of the Alternative Project were doing the "right thing."

Over the years, the sense of rightness has persisted. Certain beliefs are shared by all the Multiage teachers: children need a say in what they do; children need to be able to make some choices; children need to exercise independence; children need to experience "the conversation around the sandbox," to process in words what they've experienced; that a comfortable classroom atmosphere is important for learning to occur; a sense of common property is important to develop; and that a sense of community and one's responsibility to it are important to nurture. There is also agreement that if children are with other children who are academically inclined, they'll more easily get what they need academically and that multiage family groupings are one way of causing this to happen. (note 6) It is the strength of this shared belief system and the ways the team has realized its convictions in practice that makes Multiage such a strong unit.

There have been changes over the years. Team members talk

"The program was not imposed on the community."

25

about having to become more structured in their practice. They talk about the increased development and implementation of curriculum guidelines and the intrusion into their classroom time of other important initiatives: drug and alcohol awareness programs, computer technology programs, and increased pressures on the basics. They observe that children come to them less prepared psychologically for school. Even in this more affluent community, daily living has become more hectic as families struggle to maintain the life styles they have chosen. To these wise veterans, children seem less secure as they enter school now than they were in the beginning years of the program in the early 1970s. The teachers attribute this to fewer hours with family in the very early years. Most families have working parents and many have experienced the discontinuities that result from the separation and remarriage of parents. All this contributes to a sense of instability among their children. The teachers have to work harder to create a predictable, productive, trusting community in their classrooms. Their children's lives are more programmed with things to do and places to go. The materialism so characteristic of many families doesn't make up for the fact that the basic parental unit is less available than it used to be. The teachers express that the work they do is even more important today than perhaps it used to be because their children are less self-assured and confident, more concerned with themselves, their possessions, their place in a group. Because of all these issues they confront every day the children walk in the door, the teachers are very much present in each other's lives and they intentionally support each other's individual and collective work. Anne's work in her classroom is an extension of this team ethic just as they represent an extension of her work. They meet regularly to plan and coordinate and support each other professionally and at times, personally.

The support is necessary for another reason. Formed as an alternative in 1972, it remains an alternative now. The relationship between Multiage and the rest of the school has been an uneasy one over the years. The faculty turnover in the school mirrors the turnover in Multiage. It has been minimal. Shelburne is a school of veteran teachers and there may still be a feeling of resentment among the "regulars" because the imposition of the Multiage alternative in 1972 implied their teaching wasn't quite good enough. It was also a time when models abounded and their existence was supported as long as no one tried to make anyone else teach "my way." Whatever the reason, the team feels a kind of barrier exists between themselves and their colleagues. Most of the time it is a barrier unspoken and unarticulated. The team works at trying to be part of the entire faculty and the staff is pleasant enough with one another. As a faculty, the teachers unite in their opposition or approbation towards commonly held issues. But when faced with initiatives that suggested merging Multiage and the regular faculties

"Over the years, the sense of rightness has persisted."

26

into a Multiage-based school, tension is felt. In 1988, a bond vote was placed before the townspeople to build a new school, the architecture of which was designed to accommodate the teaching practices of Multiage classroom settings. The superintendent had aligned himself with an emerging national interest to restructure classroom grouping patterns to address issues of inequality, social incompatibility, and failing academic achievement. It was a difficult year for Anne and the team. It was a difficult year for the school faculty. The town voted "No!" on the appropriation, and the issue defused with the vote.

There have been other tensions over the years. It bothers Anne a good deal. The divergence among the faculty groups is hard for her to accept because so many of her colleagues' rooms look so much like hers. The invisible walls are the hardest ones to deconstruct.

I observe that the tension among the faculty keeps a certain intensity of purpose present among the team. They are not embattled. Neither are they fully integrated. The situation keeps them sure about what they do and present in each other's professional practice. It makes each of them more effective as teachers. Because of their unity, they have been able to retain events and practices that are important and central to their multiage teaching. Their common voice has served a political purpose in the internal resource structure of the school. It means Anne has been able to have certain multiage necessities available to her: influence in placement decisions for children in Multiage and her class; a report card appropriate for Multiage; control of large time blocks that promote child-centered activity, and the regrouping of children at times during the day among the team, Friday morning specials, mini-courses, day camp, and no morning recess time. These practices have remained part of the Multiage culture throughout the program's history.

"The teachers have to work harder to create a predictable, productive, trusting community in their classrooms."

Chapter 3

The Elements of Multiage Teaching and Learning: Adult Perspective

This issue of the Multiage team's persistence and history cuts to the avowed intent of my research. I claim that Multiage persists because it provides the kind of learning experience many parents in the community want for their children. The children who experience it thrive. Year after year, there is a waiting list of parents who want to enroll their children in this alternative. Presently, a lottery is used to fill open vacancies.

My research identifies seven elements of the teaching and learning environment in Room A, which make the multiage grouping pattern work successfully. I define those elements as I see them and as I believe the children in Anne's room experience them. The elements occur frequently and at the same time. They interact to create a richness for learning that is greater than the sum of their parts. This realization led to the addition of "overlappingness" as one of the elements.

I conclude this section realizing that Multiage can be viewed as a legitimate subculture within the larger school setting. The fact that the four classrooms share this cultural dimension creates a kind of historical momentum that has kept the program strong and viable.

These are the elements as I have come to understand them.

1. Continuity: A term used to describe classroom events in Anne's room that connect with past happenings in the lives of the children and create a setting that is familiar, known, and that has stability and predictability for them. Continuity also refers to a continuity between home and school, intentional connections between "subject matter" and children's lives, and a continuity of tradition within the Multiage rooms and across the history of Multiage. Continuity also means being in a classroom with a group of peers for more than one year. It means you know the informal and formal classroom routines. It means you are known as a child and learner for longer than one academic year.

2. Family: A term used to describe how Anne taught her students to relate to each other and to her. She modeled these behaviors as well. Family is a kind of "one for all, all for one" attitude that creates a basic understanding shared by everyone in the class that "we are all in this together." As family, the children work together, watch out for and help each other. They recognize their differences, age differences included, as normal—just like family. The age difference in Anne's room is part of the defining characteristic of "family" and "Multiage." Family was a term coined by one of the older children. It is not Anne's term.

As a category, family was created by combining two subcategories, inclusiveness ("all for one. . .") and mutuality ("we are all in this together").

3. Grouping: A term used to describe the variety of ways children gather together (self-selected) or are placed together (intentional) during the different times of the classroom day for purposes of teaching and learning. In Anne's room, many groupings are seen at any moment. Some are intentionally organized by her or the children with a specific purpose in mind, others occur naturally.

4. Informality: A term used to describe the ambiance of Anne's teaching/learning environment. As opposed to "business-like" or "formal," informality denotes classroom behaviors that are child-sensitive and respectful of a child's particular tendencies. In her informal environment, Anne's instructional tone is more conversational, the seating is rug and table oriented, and talk, rather than silence, is taken to be the currency of learning. Teacher-directed instruction is always present but usually occurs within a set of experiences that has had considerable exploration by the children. The children are shown fundamental respect as learners and teachers.

The informal nature of the setting encourages child to child and teacher to child interactions where punishment is absolutely minimized, an important element in Anne's multiage setting. As a result of the informal nature of the setting, not getting something right is perceived as one step on the path to getting something right. "Not right" is seen by the children as an inherent part of learning. Finally, the physical structure of Room A encourages small groups to gather, conversations to occur, and materials to be touched and handled. In this sense, it is an informal design, compared with a conventional room design that directs the attention of students towards the

"My research identifies seven elements of the teaching and learning environment in Room A, which make the multiage grouping pattern work successfully."

teacher and away from distracting things in the room, like each other.

5. Interaction: A term used to describe the variety of encounters, sometimes manipulated by Anne, that children have with other children, adults, places, and things in the classroom, school, and community. "Interaction" is an important element in Anne's understanding of how children learn, how they construct meaning from the world. The belief it denotes of course is that children do not learn through engagements with their world that are passive and abstract. Rather their learning is properly engaged when it is both active and focused upon things that have meaning for them.

Interaction relates to both the content and form of learning in Room A. It permits Anne's children to pursue tasks (content) in a way (form) that seems to have more value for them. This keeps motivation high and sets a tone for most of the activity that occurs in Room A.

6. Routine(s): A term used to describe those things that occur in Anne's room with regularity, usually daily. The daily schedule, expected behaviors, patterns of creating interest in the room, all these are routines. Routine(s) is also used to describe her thinking/planning framework, most notably in the study for the play. Her planning follows a routine form built through years of experience and decision making.

Interestingly enough, routine also surfaced as an element through my observation of "off-task behavior," a regular occurrence of folder work during afternoon language arts and math time.

The last example not withstanding, routines allow children to work independently and on their own because they know what is expected of them. This allows Anne time to work intentionally with smaller groupings of children, an important element in this multiage setting.

The category was formed by incorporating several subcategories into an existing routines category: the play, lunch-count questions, afternoon, thinking/planning schema, and off-task behavior.

7. Overlappingness: (note 7) A term used to describe the interdependent nature of family, interaction, grouping, continuity, routine, and informality. The power of any of the elements is in its simultaneous occurrence with other elements. Each builds upon another to establish a Multiage kind of synergy. Informality without continuity and interaction would probably lead to misbehavior.

Using material that is of interest to the children (continuity and informality), that children know about in different and shared ways (grouping), that they usually talk and write about (routine), places a value on what is to be learned. The overlapping of the elements of grouping and continuity assures there are always questions to be asked and more to be learned because the children look at things differently due to their mixed ages.

"Family is a kind of 'one for all, all for one' attitude . . . 'we are all in this together.'"

30

In Room A, the children know required skills are indirectly built into their mornings and directly built into their afternoons.

In identifying the seven elements, I reached a major goal of the study. But somehow, listing the elements in this manner didn't seem quite like the point of all this study and work. The elements, listed starkly, seemed so separated from the context out of which they were generated that they felt empty of meaning. The elements should connote richness and promise, not analysis and definition. I searched for another explanation, an explanation that would be more authentic for me.

After stewing about this turn of events and feeling increasingly despondent that my work was for naught, I gained an insight that seemed all too simple. It is one thing to explain the elements making this classroom work in adult language with adults as the audience. It would be quite another thing to explain the elements as children might describe them to adults. After all, the central characteristic of this room is a teaching/learning environment organized for the way children learn! In what is probably the most subjective leap of the entire study, I decided to try to capture each of the elements as if the children were speaking directly to them. What follows is a description of each of the seven elements as children in Room A experienced them.

The Children's Perspective

Learning the children's perspective occurred in two ways. I used semi-structured interviews. I also learned the children's interpretation of events in their room through pictures that showed them at work. First, the interviews.

During my residence in Room A I formally interviewed seven children. The interviews were carried out in the nooks and crannies of the classroom as the following note to myself describes.

> We were back by the easel, part rug area, part hardwood floor. We sat huddled in the listening center, a low tri-wall cardboard table top painted thick with layers of enamel paint, this year's version—forest green. My trusty Sony recorder, its in-place microphone like the grill of an old DeSoto, faced my two confidants. The prattle of the rest of the room surrounded us. The wind had picked up sometime between ten and noon and on this almost spring day, the windchill had dropped below zero degrees. Indoor recess, the bane of most sane teachers, had brought us together—Jimmy, Jamie, and I. I was conducting another student interview.

We'd find a place in the room, move closely together, and I'd start asking questions. Sometimes the children would face me directly, sometimes they'd face the small recorder. I used a semi-structured interview format because I knew what I wanted to ask, and I also wanted the interview to be a conversation. After the third

" . . . the children know required skills are indirectly built into their mornings and directly built into their afternoons."

interview, I arranged my questions in a format that was more or less sequential and showed it to the children as we talked. The arrangement was mostly for me, to make sure I asked all that I wanted. It was easy to get sidetracked and I was less likely to do that after I formalized the questioning routine. Figure 2 shows the format I used. It is a replica of the handwritten copy in my field notes. A portion of the children's interpretation to follow comes from the impressions I gained in these interviews. A second portion comes from their interpretation of photographs.

Figure 2

Questioning grid used in interviews with the children in Room A

2	1	3	4	5
How did you get in Multiage ?	What is your history in Multiage ?	How does Multiage work ? How does Explore Time work ?	How is Multiage unique or special ? How is it different from the "regular" ?	Is your membership in Room A or all of Multiage ?
6	7			8
What is the role of the different ages in Multiage ?	Is there a place in the room where you could take a picture that would "stand" for Multiage ?	Do you think about what you are going to do in Explore Time before school ? Do you at all ?	Do you like school ? What do you like about it ?	If a friend moved to Shelburne, what would you tell them about Multiage ?

The children of Room A weren't old enough to put the meaning of their classroom into formal, abstract language. They couldn't speak about Room A in a comparative way since most of them had no other school experience. But, they could recognize familiar and meaningful experiences of their classroom when they saw them and this realization proved to be a breakthrough in my comprehension of the children's understanding of what was happening in Room A. My clue was their responses to interview question #7: "Is there a place in the room where you could take a picture that would stand for Multiage? Where is it and what would it focus on?" To a child, they were able to respond to this question. They would hear it, often ask for clarification, look around the room and think a while, and then say something like. "I think the rug." or "Over there because that's where we all sit together." Because of their immediate responses, I decided to photograph a whole variety of events and scenes in Room A. Then during several Explore Times later on in the spring, I showed the slides to small groups of volunteers and asked them which were "typical" and why? Over several days, word spread of this new activity and I talked with perhaps twenty children. I learned they could recognize what their classroom meant to them when they saw it. They could point out areas in their classroom and classroom practices that they liked. They could tell me what they did, and they could tell me which of my photographic images of them in action were typical of Room A and why they were typical or atypical. Their easy recognition of these typical elements is important and significant information. On the next several pages are some of their responses gathered from these Explore Time showings plus a session with the whole class early in May.

"They could tell me what they did, and they could tell me which of my photographic images of them in action were typical of Room A and why they were typical or atypical."

33

"I'm going to show these slides. Tell me if you think any of them should be selected as what your room is really like."

Photo 1

No. It doesn't show anything we are doing. I like the ones that show what we build, what we draw. Like that one.

Photo 2

Yes. It shows the projects we do (also Photo 10).

Photo 3
We always build a lot of things with blocks.

Photo 4
Use that one. You can see the kind of work we do every day. (It shows a Monday morning journal.)

Photo 5

Yes, that one. It shows Mrs. Bingham and the bulletin board. (The children had made the bulletin board.)

Photo 6

I liked the one of that part of the room. I think that's the best place to get a picture of the kind of things we do. It has the calendar, Laurie's story, the lunch menu, the weather.

This is the area next to Anne's easel from which they start the day. It functions as a kind of operational center of the room. Schedules, calendar, and the like. It's kind of like the "information center" (child's term) of the room.

Photo 7

I think that one, the one of your desk. It shows the teacher is busy.

Photo 8

That one, too. The computer is an important part of the room. We do a lot on it.

Photo 9

I like the picture of the rug 'cause it showed parts of the Legos and all of the work all over there, like Sally was writing and Susie was doing math with Unifix cubes.

Photo 10

I liked the one where we were doing our Monday morning journals 'cause it showed what we were doing in the morning. (see also Photo 6)

The pictures could be a study all by themselves. In addition to being an effective catalog of the room environment, each one portrays several of the elements typical of Room A in overlapping fashion. A variety of interactions occur in the informal nature of the activities, evidence of routine, and especially in photo #2, a variety of multiage groupings. Photo 10 portrays the friendships valued so highly by the children. Photo 2 shows continuity in the batteries and bulbs work that had begun as a Friday morning special several months before.

38

Photo 10 was taken during Explore Time (as were most of the pictures chosen by the children) and shows two first-grade boys at work in the block area, a first-grade girl working hard on her writing, and a second- and third-grade girl working together on a survey/graphing activity. The girls were determining the frequency of alphabet letters occurring in the names of the eighty children in Multiage. It is a classic Explore Time scene. It communicates involvement, perspective, intensity, and pleasure.

I learned from the children that Anne's teaching and the teaching of the Multiage team persists year after year because Multiage has been a good place for children to be. They like it, their friends like it, they learn about things, they learn about people, they learn math, their writing and reading, they learn how to work, they learn how to get along with a variety of human beings, they learn self-control, and they know the same has been true for their brothers and sisters and other children of Shelburne. They also know it can be fun. They know this from both their own experience and from information passed down in the community about Multiage. These children not only bring home good messages about school, they *are* good messages about school. That's why parents have been so supportive of Multiage. One parent put it this way when she learned what I was doing:

"Should be interesting. I'll hear more about it later. I like the more professional aspect (that you're going to be looking at). Enjoy our children. They're all above average, like in Lake Wobegon."

Multiage is not perfect and it isn't always tidy. Anne will be the first one to talk about the things that go wrong, the last minute changes, what she was unsure of, her unsettled feeling of always adjusting something to make it better, how she wishes she had more time to do more of something she knows is important. But it's "good enough" and it sets a high standard for responsiveness to the needs of children.

So, what does Multiage stand for from a child's perspective? If you were a child in Room A, how would you talk about your classroom and the things you do there? What follows is a blending of comments from the children that surfaced in three ways: interviews, comments about various photographs, and comments I recorded from classroom conversations. The comments are mostly their words with my interpretations. I have placed them within the seven elements that define the teaching and learning environment.

First and foremost, Multiage is about family. The children talk about their room in terms of the relationships they have with each other. To them it is like a family. Anne once said her desire to teach multiage groupings could be wrapped up in two words: community and helping. Her use of community as a guiding principle involves the helping relationship she wants to engender among her children. Her success in doing this is seen in their acknowledging Multiage as family. The two terms are absolutely compatible in their meaning.

> "Room A is kind of like a family. Our class is different than "the regular." We have younger and older kids in here. We learn to get along together and to appreciate and use the different things we can do. It feels more natural that way. Actually sometimes it's better than family. My brother beats up on me a lot."

> "This is better. What we do, we all do. We are all respected and included in the fun things. We share the chores. When Mrs. B. says we need to get started, we all get started, even her. We all get to go on field trips although sometimes we go on separate trips because of our ages or what we are studying. The other part of the school is the regular because, well, it's sort of regular. It's only one grade and everyone's about in the same place, and they do everything at one time, together. In Multiage we do different things with our different grades but we're all included in the doing of it. We are expected to keep our room together, picked up if not entirely neat, and we work together to solve our big problems. The little ones we let Mrs. B. take care of."

> "We watch out for each other. We kind of depend on each other. Some kids are better at some things than other kids but there are no better kids in here than some other kids. I've learned what I'm good at, and what I'm not so good at and I know who to ask and where to go for help. I remember Laurie's aunt's fire and it really made me feel bad. . . ."

Multiage is also a place that is connected to things and experiences the children know about. Most things from home are allowed into the room. Some things are not (toys from the older kids and weapons of destruction from anyone). The children feel free to bring things in, talk about their families, and talk about what they are learning. These overlapping elements of continuity, informality, and interaction are highlighted in the following segment.

> "What I can do in here has something to do with things I've done before. I can bring in things from home that interest me. Almost always I can talk about them and usually I can use them in the classroom, even if its only to write about them. My brother was in Multiage and he liked it a lot. We also work on things in here over days, sometimes even weeks. We've been studying foods now for two months. I get a little tired of it, but I've learned a lot about seeds and leaves, and fruits and grains. Did you know that you can grow grains? We did it the day after we made frozen yogurt. It tasted really good. I played with Jerry after school last week and we told his mother about it. We made it at home. It was better at school."

Beyond family, the children talked most frequently about "doing things." Doing things was their most frequently invoked criteria of accepting or rejecting a given photograph of them in their room and it refers to the learning environment as they experienced it in Room A. To them, learning is doing.

Learning is informal and fun. (routines, interaction, grouping, informality)

"There are lots of ways to learn things in here. We talk a lot. We draw a lot. We can sit at tables or sit on the rug. There are plenty of times when we can talk to our friends about what we are doing and get help from them. I like hearing about what my friends have done. It gives me lots of ideas about things to do. There is also a time every day when I can do exactly what I want to do. I can even go to another multiage room and do something there. I usually meet my friends and we decide to play a game or build airplanes or play with the computer. I have to be able to explain what I'm doing when Mrs. B. comes around. Sometimes that's hard. My favorite thing is to make spaceships with the fancy cubes."

Learning is anticipatory. (interaction, continuity, grouping, informality)

"I'm in a class where I can watch my friends learning things I don't know how to do yet. It goes on all the time. I can listen to what they are doing while I'm doing my work and kinda practice what it's going to be like before I have to do it. I've been watching Jeff do his math with Mrs. B. and I think I could play that chip game right now. I'm not sure what it means, but I think I could play the game."

I like to learn in this way. (grouping, interaction, informality)

"Jeffrey and I decided to go for the record in tower building. We got all the Cuisenaire rods that we could and started building. I was nervous! The tower got so high! Some kids from Room B came in and tried to knock it down by stamping their feet next to it. Mandy came over and stopped them. She really wanted us to get it. We got giggling when we put the last small pieces on top and I thought we were going to knock it over. Explore Time was over before we were sure about the record. I think we did it. It was fun to pull out one piece on the bottom and watch it collapse. Everyone loved the sound."

Learning is sometimes hard. (routines, interaction, grouping)

"Today I was working on my math. I had to do these subtraction problems where I had to borrow. I don't get it. Sometimes I forget and can't understand what happens. I can do it on my fingers but when I use the numerals it doesn't work for me. Later in the afternoon Mrs. B. played Bankers Three-For-One with me and Jimmy. I felt good about doing that but I don't see how it helps me with my subtracting numbers. It feels like I can't do the important stuff." (interaction, grouping)

"I'm in a class where I can watch my friends learning things I don't know how to do yet."

41

I have time to learn things and learn them better. (continuity, interaction)

"I thought is was really neat to hear the third graders talk about that tree stump where we meet on the playground. They were here when it was a real tree and they can remember sitting under its shade. I brought a bunch of maple helicopters in from the playground. We're going to try and sprout them in the room. I'll take some home to try them at home too. They are seeds just like the seeds we've been studying in the unit on foods. Mrs. B. brought up a bunch of books on seeds and trees from the library. I wonder if they are about the playground tree?"

Learning is carried out in many ways, often intensely. (interaction, informality, grouping)

"I like to do things in order and I like them to be neat. I often use a ruler and my sharp pencil and I work hard at what I'm doing. I want it to be right. Not everyone is like me. At my table today we were trying to draw this still life of fruit. We had to see if we could get the shadow right and show where the light was reflecting off from it. I used my pencil. Adam was using a crayon. Mark was using the Pentels. Bobby was using crayon and pencil. At the other table, Mandy was using chalk. When we had our afternoon circle, we had to show the group our drawing and explain what we were trying to do and how it went. It was a whole lot easier for me to talk about it than to do it. I didn't like the smudges on my paper. I'm going to write about it in my journal because it frustrates me. Maybe I'll even do a story about how the fruit felt."

By design, Anne's room is an informal learning setting (Figure 1, Page 5). It is a challenge to keep the ambiance informal and focused on activities of interest that also serve academic purposes. Anne has to work hard to provision a setting in which the children feel comfortable. Their comfort is heard in the humor between teacher and child, the shared jokes, her sensitivity to real-life happenings, her gentle touch on even the most challenging of children, and the conversational tone that dominates discourse in the classroom.

There were so many conversations among children during a given day that I could not come close to identifying how many. Suffice it to say that the conversational atmosphere in the room is dense. It is dense in both the quantity and quality of conversations. Here is a sample of talk between a first grader and a second grader while they played with Multiplex cubes, better known as "the fluorescent cubes." As they talked, their hands moved rapidly, creating and transforming airplane shapes with surprising speed.

Adam: "I got thirteen on the wing. I need two here."
Roger: "My tail's not sticking up here."
Adam: "What do you mean? You're doing it right."
Roger: "No, Adam. See, you do it like this."

Roger, two years younger than Adam, leaves and cruises momentarily around the room with his jet. Adam places several cubes more on his construction. Then the other boy comes back.

He holds his airplane up, regards it with a studying look. They both smile.

Adam: "It's not quite right."

I ask what it is.

Adam: "A jet."

Roger: "Can I have a yellow one?"

Adam: "No."

I ask if they have a plan they are following. They look at me with a bit of exasperation in their eyes.

Adam: "No, I made this up (shows me his jet which I now understand is the model) and he's following it."

In my initial analysis of the quality of conversation for this short interaction, I listed the following potential categories:

- play with pretend objects,
- kid language,
- spontaneous conversation not available to the teacher,
- statements of fact, question, affirmation, judgment, and declaration,
- child rejecting another child's idea,
- child demonstrating with a model he's made,
- protection of space,
- externalizing the thought process with language,
- researcher searching for label,
- researcher searching for process,
- learning through looking, and
- looking in for the kindergartner who kept walking by watching what was going on

The entire study could have been done on two days' worth of recording and observation at this micro level of analysis! In the end, this sequence was categorized as "interaction," "verbal," "child to child," "grouping," and "older modeling learning for younger." Informality allowed this kind of talk to happen. When it did, it was complex.

Even Anne's warnings to get her children back on task have a conversational nature to them: "We aren't doing very well with this, are we?" Or, "Hey you guys, be quiet! I want to hear this!"

All the different types of learning the children identified in the pictures have informality as a fundamental characteristic. Many of the learnings continue from day to day so the children pick up on activities with which they already have a history. Continuity is a major characteristic of this environment and, like family, it often is seen in the informal nature of the room as well.

The interactions in Anne's room are frequent and take many different forms. Interaction is the stuff of learning in this room.

"Interaction is the stuff of learning in this room."

43

What the children know and learn about is most frequently learned from encounters with things in the classroom. Rarely are they required to mentally compose something without any processing of the information. The interactive processing takes place between and among children, children and teacher, and children and things. The children's overall descriptor of Room A as a room where "we do things" comes from the frequency of social and physical interactions. The Classroom Study provided many instances of these kinds of interactions. The following list comes from a fourteen minute period one morning after Anne purposefully assigned children to tables and ended circle by reminding them of the ways they could be helpful with each other. Most of these are multiage interactions. They are examples of academically oriented behaviors (for the most part) and behaviors of helpfulness characteristic of family.

1. Mandy asks Betsy for help in deciding what she should make.
2. Ray asks Alan to sharpen his pencil.
3. Betsy asks me how to spell "yesterday." Mandy says, "That's easy." I tell Betsy to check with Mandy.
4. Susie ends up spelling it for her in her wordbook.
5. Lindy and Stephanie are talking about a hat. "Lindy, will you help me draw a hat?"
6. Jimmy and his mom (in to help with Monday morning journals) are discussing the short "a" sound.
7. Mandy needs the word "expedition." She talks to Susie about how to spell it and then goes and gets her wordbook to make the entry.
8. Ray tells Mark to start working.
9. Stephanie asks me to help her erase something by holding the paper.
10. Lindy helps Stephanie draw a hat. Once done, Stephanie erases it and goes and draws it herself.
11. The girls and boys at table one are talking about the new babies coming into several families in this class.

"You got a sister?"
"No, I got a brother."
"I found out it will be a girl."
"How?"
"My mom took a test."
"Is that its picture?"
"Uh huh."
"Babies are very small."
"You need a date on that."

12. Mike is struggling with this assignment. Anne rubs his back and helps him form a wordbook. "What was the other sound?"

"W. It's like a wobble-u to me."

13. Cindy and Jimmy talk about Jimmy's pictures of the baby soon to arrive at his home. She's talking about her little sister. "She takes after my mom's feet."

14. Stephanie goes to Susie for help. Susie sends her for scrap paper. Writes "this" and the day's date.

15. Susie shares with me that this is her first time writing cursive. Last Thursday she finished all her lower case letters. She did it during the afternoon language arts block. I tell her I used to write more neatly. This study was causing my writing to decline noticeably.

16. Jerry to Jamie and Ethan: "I wrote ten letters!" Jamie and Ethan clap.

Interaction is the primary medium through which a significant amount of learning occurs in this room; it is the "doing things" of learning. Anne plans it that way. The children magnify its impact because they help each other. After all, it's family.

I've noted two reasons why Multiage persists: the elements that combine to make it successful from an adult point of view, and how children may experience those elements. The two interlock but are not the same. I believe there is a third reason. It has to do with the notion that Multiage is its own subculture within the larger school environment. The rituals, customs, and shared meanings unique to Multiage appear in this vignette.

> One day on the way to lunch, we were walking past the kitchen window in the basement hallway. I walked beside Mark, Jimmy, and Alan. I was shuffling my way to lunch when they pointed to the floor and shouted to me, "Don't step on the crack! Alligators!" I jumped, startled by the suddenness of their demands. Seemed like there were alligators under the floor and if I stepped on the crack in the pavement, I'd meet them firsthand. Jimmy piped in that there were "cooties" there as well. After lunch I pursued the issue of the alligators a bit. Seemed like this was a Multiage joke. To the best of their knowledge, none of the kids in the regulars knew about the alligators and cooties—only the kids in Multiage.

The children share a common set of values, rituals, and patterns of behavior, and they even share jokes about hidden alligators and cooties. The shared meanings and events all denote the fact that the history of Multiage since 1972 has seen the creation of a rather distinct subculture separate and apart from the dominant regular culture. Cultures, like organizations, tend to persist across time because of the complexity of their interlocking cultural mores. The momentum of history contributes to Multiage's persistence.

"The children share a common set of values, rituals, and patterns of behavior . . ."

Chapter 4

Anne's Teaching: How She Does It

I have had many occasions to talk about multiage teaching and learning to groups of teachers and parents. There are always those in the audience for whom the concept is not only new, it is distasteful. It goes against everything they know or believe or have experienced as schooling. I can spot the question coming by the manner of slouch in a chair, the talk back and forth with a spouse or colleague, the increase in knitting speed as yet another row of a grandchild's sweater is gained. The question raised is usually polite enough, often after a little speech about a friend's child who wasted a year in second grade "playing around." It goes something like this: "But why would anyone want to teach that way?" The statements behind the question are really two:

1. "Teaching like that takes too much time and work."
2. "Children really can't be trusted to learn that way."

Of central importance in Anne's ability to teach the way she does is the support of her team and the momentum of their practice over the history of Multiage. Also, Anne has a point of view about what needs to happen with children in our society. This point of view is fundamental to the way she brings children into the world of subject matter and required content. It is consistent with her practice. Her view of herself as teacher is less as a transmitter of knowledge than as a participant in the creation of knowledge. She teaches knowledge directly when she understands that children need the information she is giving to them.

"Ethan is ahead of the others now. He actually spent another year at the first grade level, but he's needed to sit in on all the times we've given phonics instruction, structure, and review. Now, he's just gone over a hump and he's gone! Kids do that. They go over a

46

hump and all of a sudden they are independent readers."

Everyone in Anne's classroom is a capable learner and everyone learns, even her. Her room is organized to enable each child to know that he or she is a learner and every friend in the classroom is a learner. Anne can do what she does because she is a learner, constantly playing off what she sees being constructed and learned by her children.

The diversity of the multiage setting promotes her basic vision.

"I see them as a group of kids who are developmentally at lots of different places and there are two important things that happen. One is that I see them that way. I don't see them as a bunch of second graders who should all be doing second-grade work or that they should be writing something specific right now. I can't think that way, it's impossible. That's one thing.

"The other thing is the way they bounce off each other all the time. That is probably different. The way they work together and are able to model things for each other. Once in a while I'll ask one child to work with another, read to another or hear another child, but most of the time it's children at different levels working together (and that) happens informally and naturally."

She has organized the physical space of her classroom and the pattern of her day to create a setting that fosters the dispositions of her children to help and reinforces her belief that it is possible. Anne's two fundamental reasons for teaching multiage groups are community and helping. Teaching children to live within a classroom community, or family as the children saw it, fosters their readiness to help each other. But their helping is not always direct. An important part of her environment is being in the midst of children learning, who help themselves to the learning going on among other children or between a child and Anne. She observes this situation going on all the time. Here's part of a piece she wrote for me about learning by eavesdropping so I could better understand what she meant by the term.

Three children, second and third graders, were seated doing a word puzzle about dairy products (part of the foods unit). Anne found them a challenging puzzle in her files, and they had, she said, "accepted the challenge with unmistakable excitement." They checked frequently with her as they came up with items such as evaporated milk and yogurt.

During this time there was a fourth member of the group whom I observed with interest. Mary Lou, a first grader, was sitting at the same table and very close to the other three. She was coloring a dot-to-dot cow. As she produced a fine black and white Holstein, complete with bright pink udder and surrounded by large yellow raindrops, she watched and listened. She was obviously dividing her attention between her picture and the other girls. I don't think she said a word, but she was in the midst of this word find

"Anne's two fundamental reasons for teaching multiage groups are community and helping."

47

excitement for forty minutes. Her eyes constantly flitted between her picture and the others. She was obviously engaged, and what a model she had of excitement over reading, words, and their meaning. She participated vicariously in an activity which she can look forward to participating in herself before long. The tools of reading, with which she was currently struggling, could obviously be fun, and useful in playful contexts beyond story reading, too.

Anne's belief in and use of a wide variety of developmental levels is illuminated in her story about Mary Lou.

The vignette has further use in understanding her participation in the overlapping events and elements in her room at any one time. These elements don't exist separately and sequentially. They are present at the same time during different moments in the daily schedule. In the example of learning by eavesdropping, there is the simultaneous existence of continuity (another event in the foods unit, Mary Lou's continuing mastery in learning to read), informality (the girls being allowed to work and talk together, Sarah being a girl from another room, two very different activities going on at the same table), interaction (thought and language, crayon and paper, within student groups, across student groups, student to teacher), learning as fun, challenge, anticipation, and hard work, and Anne's resourcefulness—she located spontaneously a word challenge filed away in the not-too-recent past that was just right for the three girls at that moment. And significantly, Anne is able to deal with lots of things going on at the same time. Her classroom is a place where multiple activities occur during common time frames much of the day. Theme time, Explore Time, language arts and math time, are all structured parts of her day organized to permit multiple activities with multiple sources of learning. She is also able to focus on one or two children during these multiple activity times and teach them in the way they need a teacher. She teaches Betsy and Frank about regrouping and place value through chip trading while the rest of her class fulfills their weekly math contracts.

The example provides evidence of yet another characteristic of Anne as a teacher. She is highly reflective about her work. Her reflectiveness is done within "the big picture" of her beliefs and what she wants to occur for her children. It permits the children independence and resourcefulness and allows her to nurture these tendencies through her organization of classroom and subject mat-ter. Her reflectiveness is also a perspective on her career. Though she has been in Multiage since 1972, not one year has ever been the same as another.

Inside and Outside Perspectives

Early in my days of observation, I gave Anne a copy of my transcribed notes. I had reflected that I wasn't sure where I was seeing "reading instruction" occurring. I was seeing reading going on in all kinds of ways, but I my was wondering where kids were getting help learning to read. The question came from my attempt to understand what I was and wasn't seeing. In our next interview, Anne responded:

> I have a feeling that you haven't seen much and maybe you don't know what you're seeing exactly. You know a year-long picture is important sometimes and you stepped in in February. You know I did use basals for a long, long time. I never used the manuals, never used them as a basal but in an individualized way. And I did use the workbooks for a long time but never in any traditional way. I have always wanted to do something different and I have tried things and not been satisfied and tried something else and not been satisfied. And I'm not satisfied with a totally individualized reading program partly because of the amount of research that's come out in the last few years about comprehension and you need to pre-read like you need to pre-write, you need to talk about things ahead of time to help 'prime the pump' and you need to show kids how to predict. There's a lot you can do that kids don't do if they work individually. I've made a gradual shift in stops and starts to doing mostly literature and I'm using a literature based reading series right now. And so what I'm trying to say is that every year I've gone just a little bit differently. I'm in constant revision. It's awfully hard work to do it that way but it's never boring. Right now I'm working so hard on getting the writing process started and rolling that you haven't seen much reading.

This is a teacher who has been refining her program for the length of her career. The refinement has not occurred by adopting fads. The refinement has occurred because of her thoughtful, reflective nature. As researcher, I parachuted into the midst of a stream of moments. I raised questions about those moments. But they were also not-too-veiled statements about Anne's teaching as well. Because of the trust between us as collaborators, she was able to come back to me and clarify what I was seeing. As researcher, I walked into the middle of a career, into the middle of an ongoing unit of study, into the middle of twenty individual relationships between teacher and students, into the middle of this week's plan for Sally or Mary Lou or any other child in the classroom. Each moment I observed was just that, a moment in the time and space of Room A. It was also a moment in the dimensionality of Anne's career and her ongoing reflective process as a professional educator. At the time, I saw my presence in Room A as one moment in a layered set of interlocking histories (see Figure 3 next page).

"Her reflectiveness keeps her growing in insight and new knowledge and in her ability to see her children individually and collectively."

Figure 3

Journal entry concerning Anne's career and my observations

Notes on the day after Anne Bingham read my first package of field notes. The labels are mine, placed after the conversation.

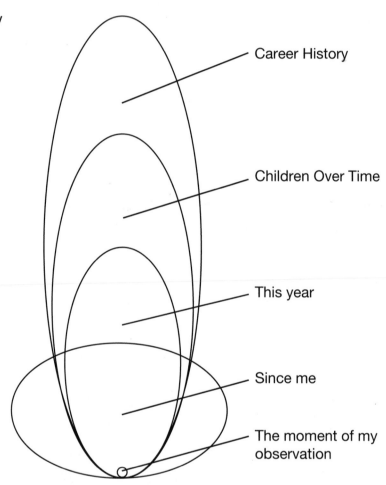

Career History

Children Over Time

This year

Since me

The moment of my observation

In my moment of observation, I miss the various histories associated with what I see. I am blind to the growing edges and my observations become ill-informed judgments on the career growth of a teacher. Think what this means relative to qualitative data and its power to condense meaning.

Her reflectiveness keeps her growing in insight and new knowledge and in her ability to see her children individually and collectively. It also keeps her researcher colleague humble and honest about his compulsion to learn about the happenings in Room A and not to impose his own conclusions about what he sees.

Finally, Ann manages to do her work because she knows a lot of information about many things and the structure of her day permits her opportunities to use her knowledge indirectly as well as directly. When she listens to children read or helps three children with the mystery of regrouping in double-digit subtraction, that's the direct use of her knowledge. The indirect use of what she knows occurs at surprising times and with stunning sensitivity.

One morning, Alan brought a tightly taped shoe box to opening circle .

> Anne: "Alan, bring that over. It's a very well-taped box, isn't it. Is it something fragile?"
> Alan: "Not really. Yeah, sort of, sort of."
> Anne: "Is it a model?"
> Alan: "It's something from the poem."
> Anne: "From the poem I read?"
> Alan: "Yeah, you just read."

Anne had just read the poem "Dreams" by Langston Hughes. She had been preparing the children for an African-American author who was coming to the school.

Alan carefully opens the box and unwraps an object fully enclosed in a wrapping of toilet paper. No one even comments on the toilet paper. They are riveted to his actions. He's a boy who's been almost hidden in the class. Recently, he's become more prominent because he's taught a whole slew of kids how to fold paper throwing stars during Explore Time. I think the presence of this box now has something to do with the status he's achieved in the past few weeks with the throwing stars.

> From the class: "Oooh myyyy."
> "It's a dead bird."
> "Ohh my goodness."
> "Let's see. I can't see."
> "What is it? All I see is newspaper."
> Anne: "Let me help you with that. I don't want the rest of you to handle that because a dead bird sometimes has germs on it, but. . ."
> "I can't see!"
> Anne: "I can put it out where we can see it. Wait, let's give Alan some time to tell us all about it and how he got it and then you can ask your questions. Tell us what it is?"
> Alan kind of stammers inaudibly.
> "I can't see it."
> "I can't see it either."

Anne: "Well. Oh dear. You can't, can you? Okay. (Anne takes the bird from Alan and begins to show it to the class herself). Is that better? Does any one know what it is? Do you, Alan?"

Alan: "A waxwing?"

Anne: "It's a cedar waxwing."

"Ouuuu."

"Gosh."

Anne: "It's called a "cedar" and maybe while I'm carrying it around. . . "

Sally: "Why's it called that?"

Anne: "It's called that, Sally, because these little spots of yellow and red on the wings somebody thought looked a little bit like wax. It's a beautiful bird. Do you see? I'm going to carry it around. Do you see it has a black mask over its eyes? And look at its wings."

There is much talk and interest. The children are rapt with attention and staring at the beautiful dead creature that has suddenly come into their midst.

Anne: "Now while I bring it around, Alan, tell us what happened to this bird."

Alan: "There was a bug on the window and, um, it got it was like it was air and there's glass there and it didn't see it was on a glass window, or it saw it too late, and it went into the glass."

"So it rammed its head into the glass thinking it could go right through?" (Another child.)

"The bird died?" (Another child.)

Anne: "The bones in its neck broke and that's why the bird died. It's a beautiful bird. It has soft feathers, very soft."

Jerry: "Talking about birds, I. . . "

Anne: "Just a minute, Jerry. Alan, what are you going to do with it?"

Alan: "Umm, my mom said after school, umm, I shouldn't bring it home. You should throw it away because it will begin to smell real bad otherwise."

Anne: "I think maybe I'll take it out in my woods and bury it. I think I'd like to do that."

"It will make a tree. "(Another child.)

"No it won't!"

"Remember that book about Barney?"

"Yeah."

"The Tenth Good Thing About Barney"?

"Yeah, that's it. They buried him. It helped the flowers grow."

Anne: "What happened to Barney down under the earth? Bobby?"

Bobby: "He started to decompose."

Anne: "He became part of the soil and helped the flowers grow. Maybe this nice cedar waxwing will decompose into the earth and help things grow out in my yard. I'll take it home and bury it if your mother doesn't want it to come back. These birds often travel in flocks. You usually see not just one cedar waxwing but a whole lot of them and they come to places where there are berries on bushes."

Alan: "I know what you mean. We have those bushes next to our house. "

Anne: "Okay, we can lay it up here for the morning. It won't begin to smell but it would be better if people didn't handle it probably. You know, when I was a little girl, my father was a biologist who studied birds and we also had dead birds in our refrigerator."

 (A universal "Ouuu!" from the class.)

Anne: "They had been stuffed for the university so that there was a collection of birds for people to look at."

Jerry: "Now can I go? Now can I go?"

Anne: "Jerry, you had something to say about birds? Ray, we need to hear Jerry first."

Anne's classroom structure made it possible for Alan to willingly bring in the bird to show his classmates. Explore Time activities had most likely opened the door for his confidence to allow him to do so. And Anne's knowledge and sensitivity about dealing with beautiful lifeless form created a moment in time that in another place could have gone quite differently. And there was something in this poem that gave Alan the moment of entry.

> Hold fast to dreams.
> If dreams die
> life is a broken winged bird
> that cannot fly.
> Hold fast to dreams
> for when dreams go
> life is a barren field
> frozen in time.
>
> Langston Hughes

"And there was something in this poem that gave Alan the moment of entry."

Part Two

The Writing Study

The Writing Project was carried out to provide a second lens to view the teaching and learning environment in Room A. Broadly cast, I was curious to see if the classroom organization of other multiage classroom teachers might correspond to what I observed in Room A.

I also wanted to use the opportunity of working with a second set of teachers to look at a secondary question that emerged during the classroom study. During my time in Room A, I began to wonder if there was there a connection between the multiage setting I was experiencing and the research based on cooperative learning (Johnson and Johnson, 1991)? Cooperative learning has been promoted as a technique of working with diverse ability groupings of children that consistently shows higher achievement, better attitudes towards teachers and school, and more positive social relationships among children as a result of its use. Yet Anne didn't mention using cooperative learning at all. I was curious about the absence of the term, and whether children might be served differently if Anne saw herself using cooperative learning strategies. I also wondered if the other multiage teachers dealt with cooperative learning in the same way.

Some of my wondering has to do with the age of Multiage at the Village School. That practice is rooted in a belief system grounded in the developmental traditions of the British Infant Schools, a movement that grew during the 1930s and which achieved its most recent form during the post-Plowden decade starting in the mid-1960s. In recent years, a strong and reliable research base has been established for cooperative learning (Johnson and Johnson, 1991), peer tutoring (Miller, 1990) and other multiple grouping strategies (Cohen, 1989) and the team seemed quite insulated from it all. They talk a good deal about "learning cooperatively," "classroom as community," and "children helping one another" as part of their teaching framework, but they are almost disdainful of intentionally incorporating elements of these more recently established techniques into their practice.

"I don't use the term peer tutoring at all. You hear about peer tutoring all the time and I never use the term. I never think about it, and I rarely ever do anything formally. (In here) children at different levels working together happens informally and naturally."

At one point during the classroom study I even wondered out loud to Anne if the multiage learning in her room might not be strengthened with more intentional planning of mixed-age involvement. (note 8)

I considered two ways to deal with the issue. The first was to assume that the cooperative learning and peer tutoring techniques were derivative from the practice I observed in Room A and to assume the more prescribed form of cooperation called "cooperative learning," as opposed to learning cooperatively, would be a regression of practice for Anne. Adopting this point of view would make the case moot.

The second way would be to see if teachers who began teaching in the span of time since the Multiage team began their work had a different perspective on cooperative learning and peer tutoring strategies. Did their practice reflect a more intentional use of those strategies? I chose the second route.

In summary then, the purpose of The Writing Project was to gain a perspective on the elements of multiage teaching and learning that evolved in the Classroom Study. I would also use the writings to seek more information about the issue of cooperative learning that evolved in the Classroom Study.

Chapter 5

Story, Epiphany, and the Writers

I am increasingly interested in using the recall of events in one's life (life story) as a form of qualitative inquiry. In my professional life as a teacher educator, I know that practicing teachers respond more openly and willingly to colleagues' stories about their lives as teachers than they do to the facts and figures of conventional educational research. I believe this interpretation of "story" is associated with Norman Denzin's (1989) notion of interpretive interactionism.

"As a distinctly qualitative approach to social research, interpretive interactionism attempts to make the world of lived experience directly accessible to the reader. . . .

"The focus of interpretive research is on those life experiences that radically alter and shape the meanings persons give to themselves and their life projects. This existential thrust sets this research apart from other interpretive approaches that examine the more mundane, taken-for-granted properties and features of everyday life. It leads to a focus on 'epiphany.'"

Most teachers, including me, experience events in our classrooms that signify in a manner beyond pure reason what teaching is all about for us. These events include reason, but the experience is emotional and heart-felt as well. These moments are instances of heightened feeling and meaning, perhaps even of absolute confirmation of why we do what we do as teachers. These moments affirm our existence, our work, our life's work. I would judge these events to be the "moments of epiphany" to which Denzin refers. They do not hold life-challenging or threatening qualities Denzin attributes to his epiphanies, but I believe they serve the same ends. For teachers who experience these moments, the moments do shape the meaning we give to ourselves and our "life projects." Maxine Greene (1988) captures the meaning of these experiences when she argues powerfully for us to pay more attention to the narrative voice.

"We who are teacher educators need to direct our attention now and then to memory and lived life. If we do so, we cannot but summon up visions of the landscapes that ground our own and our students' life-stories, out of which each one's quest for the valuable, the worthwhile, and the meaningful must begin. . . . If thoughtfulness is important to us in more than a limited formal sense, there must be room for the interpretive, the grounded, the perspectival, the qualitative."

The Writing Project is qualitative inquiry grounded in the narrative voice of teachers writing about events in their teaching that I call epiphanies. I invited five multiage classroom teachers to write about events in their classrooms that held significant meaning for their teaching lives, special events that were "definitional" about themselves as teachers—events that confirmed their beliefs about what teaching could be and what they sought to do as teachers. From the ongoing discussion of their writings, we created a list of elements that defined their conditions of successful multiage teaching and learning. Through this process, I created more information to better understand what I had seen in Room A and to determine if my concern about cooperative learning in that multiage practice had any particular importance.

In retrospect, I made two important decisions before the writing project began. First was deciding who would be the writers. Second was deciding to hire a writing consultant.

I asked teachers to participate whom I knew to be excellent teachers of multiage classroom settings. Anne was one of the teachers. It was important to have her work represented as part of the team's effort because her comments and reflections in the first part of the study were primarily verbal. The writing voice is a different voice than the speaking voice and I wanted Anne to have a writing voice as well, a voice unencumbered by the moment-to-moment swirl of events in her classroom.

Five teachers were invited, five agreed to participate. We were our own multiage group. The age difference among us was close to a quarter of a century and no one of us had less than five years of multiage teaching experience. I knew them as gifted classroom practitioners and articulate speakers about the value of multiage classrooms. Each had lamented the lack of published materials on multiage practice. Several had said they'd like to be involved in writing about multiage if the opportunity ever arose. One (Anne) had publications to her credit. They knew each other more by reputation than by actual fact. Each used process writing in her classroom as a valued link in making the reading-writing-speaking connection for children.

I invited a sixth teacher to work with us as writing consultant. She was a gifted journalist herself, had taught courses in the process method of writing and was currently the reading specialist for a local school district. She had been an elementary teacher before extending her career into the more specific area of reading and language arts. Her presence enabled me to listen and enter into the dialogue of the writing team. The responsibility for leading the team through the writing project was hers.

The writing team met only six times: once in April, May, June, July, August, and November. At our first meeting we laid out the scope of our work so we might establish commitment to the project by the second meeting. One member felt her family would suffer if she gave the time to her writing that she envisioned. She excused herself from the team. The remaining four "signed on" for the duration of the project and decided to call themselves the Writing Collaborative. Our meetings lasted four to five hours except the July meeting, a two-day retreat, where we met almost constantly. In our early meetings we talked about our work and were led through journaling exercises to engage both our memories and our pens. In May, we agreed to read some of what we had written at our April meeting. In June, we decided to bring finished drafts to the July retreat. Our process was very much in keeping with conventions of the writing process. We wrote, we conferenced, we read to each other, we suggested changes in our work, we risked exposure. In these early sessions I took notes for the group. At the retreat I wrote several pieces about my university teaching as a multiage classroom. In many ways I participated in the group but I was clearly not "of the group." After the July and August meetings, various members of the Collaborative conferenced about their pieces by phone or in person. Our final meeting in November saw yet another round of revisions and the final drafts came to me by December.

It was an incredibly powerful process for everyone concerned but especially for the four teachers. The dialogue deepened as they revealed their visions of teaching, their moments of triumph and frustration, their inability to understand colleagues who lacked their understanding about how to be with children. They uncovered the common belief that schools can be better places for children and that their ways of teaching make schools better places for children. At first they were reluctant to tell their stories. They didn't want to preach. They knew the uselessness of trying to change others by talking at them. And they were very uncomfortable with the "I" that emerged in their stories.

"It seemed so, well, conceited. Like I'm telling teachers what they should be doing and that I've got all the answers. Lord knows I don't have all the answers. But there is a part of me that feels like, 'Yes. I do!' Schools need to be with children in quite a different fashion. I feel a certain obligation to do this."

The "I" that emerges in their collective stories is filled with the humility of knowing that every teacher's struggle to do good work is

"I invited five multiage classroom teachers to write about events in their classrooms that held significant meaning for their teaching lives . . ."

personal, unique to the individual, and known in its richest form only to that teacher. Their "I" reaches out to say, "This is the way it really is for me. How is it for you? How can it be for you? Is there a difference?" They came to realize that self-reference was only the first step in creating discourse with others. And significantly, discourse with others became their intent. My purpose for having them be together was clearly secondary to them. Their real interest was to use their writing to understand their own practice at a more fully understood level and to talk to others about their practice in all its richness and uncertainty.

They see teaching as a series of actions defined by absolute reciprocity between teaching and learning, teacher and learner, adult and child. They see themselves as "learner" as much as "teacher" and they are seen by their children as learners in their own classrooms. This became a defining characteristic of their group.

They also did not want to appear "expert." Not getting it quite right, things going wrong, getting frustrated and even angry with a child, ending up someplace other than where you wanted to go, dealing much more in the moment than following a stepwise plan, these are all occurrences in their daily teaching lives. They too have awful days and rotten moments. It's just that these awful moments aren't what's being written about here because they are not "definitional." Their stories are of the events that define the way they want their practice to be when "it's working."

A good story wraps itself around our minds and our hearts and changes us. That's why human beings have told stories seemingly forever. In the exchange comes a fuller understanding of what it is to be human, what it is to be you, what it is to be me. Coles (1989) speaks of one of his students living with fictional characters long past the time they've closed the cover on the final page of a "good read." A good story has the power to get within and become part of our experience. A character, real or imagined, who raises issues, asks questions, and confirms actions emerges to be a live presence in our lives. The group wrote for themselves. But they also wrote so that other teachers might be drawn into their work and see themselves as characters in the story of teaching that confirm, provoke, even persuade.

The Collaborative's hope is that the stories might resonate with the life experiences of other teachers, they might encourage colleagues to begin (or continue) to teach with children and learning at the center of their efforts. Their hope is that their stories of decision making would help others understand how to accomplish similar ends in their own rooms. That is my hope as well. I also hope that we identify a set of elements that define the practice, belief, and values embodied in their writings.

"A good story wraps itself around our minds and our hearts and changes us."

Chapter 6

The Characteristics of Multiage Teaching and Learning: The Teacher's Perspective

The focus upon characteristics of successful multiage teaching and learning entered our conversations at the first meeting of the Collaborative. It was impossible to talk about good practice without identifying the characteristics that caused it. The characteristics kept shifting as the writing continued. The shift wasn't a disagreement about category. It was more the process of progressively including elements into increasingly common categories to account for most cases of successful practice.

At the end of the two-day retreat, the group reviewed their writings and created the following list of eleven characteristics that seemed to hold everyone's agreement.

1. The Teacher Has a Perspective Centered in Child Responsive Learning. The teacher has a particular perspective about the relationship between diversity in student grouping and the learning of each individual in the group. They trust children to be capable learners, each in his or her own way. They know why teaching mixed-age groupings is a good thing to do. And they know that their teaching isn't always perfect nor do they believe that it must always be so. It is much more a process than a performance. They understand and exercise the relationship between teaching and learning. Their perspective is fastened on learning, not achievement. They see this as an important distinction.

2. The Teacher Is Both Teacher and Learner. These teachers see teaching and learning as all of one piece, two sides of the same coin. They share themselves as learners as well as teachers and are perceived to do so by their students. They talk about "authentic teaching" and what they mean by this is that they see themselves as learners. They know their students have things to teach them. They are not concerned when they lack knowledge of something in the classroom. They want to model a process of learning themselves for their students. They believe their students can serve as teachers in their classrooms and they create a classroom setting that encourages that kind of sharing. This means there must be plans for what they want to have happen and they must be ready to spontaneously adjust to learning situations that are inspired by their students.

3. The Teacher Plans for Spontaneous Moments. The writers talk about teaching with a kind of "routine flexibility." They see the ability to organize a routine in the classroom as an important one. Well established routines enable them to do things with groups of children while the rest of the group is otherwise engaged. They also know that unpredictable events are often of great moment. Children create lots of unplanned moments for good things to occur. Teachers in multiage settings must be able to shift gears rapidly so much so that "flexibility becomes a kind of routine for them." For these reasons, their settings often appear informal. Informal settings promote flexible planning. They know that the unplanned event is often one that is highly motivating to a child or group of children. Therefore, they build open-ended work times into their schedule. These work times are often project oriented and often begin with highly structured directions. The children then take over how the project gets carried out and make it their own. Open-ended projects, highly structured at the beginning, work in classrooms where there are children coming at their work from many different abilities.

4. The Teacher Uses Open-Ended Activity Times Intentionally. Because they value children as capable learners, the writers use open-ended activity times to observe what children do and how they do it. Watching the children at work on their self-selected activities gives the teachers valuable information about each child's interests and self-selected style of learning. The teachers then extend these activities or design units of study that will take advantage of what they have observed about their students. This creates a classroom setting where the predominant mode is interest, not disinterest. They recognize that children enter activity with feelings as well as thoughts. They also understand the value of time in pursuing an interest.

5. The Teacher Plans for Learning That Runs Deep. The writers understand learning to be something besides an accomplishment. "Real learning" has a quality of personal confirmation for the learner. It is an event that occurs deeply within an individual. It is a personal confirmation. To achieve the potential for this kind of

"These teachers see teaching and learning as all of one piece, two sides of the same coin."

61

learning, time needs to be controlled. When an activity is going well, it's kept going. The purpose for open-ended time blocks is the potential for this kind of wholly absorbed learning event.

6. The Teacher Values and Promotes Wholeness. "Wholeness" is one of those terms that perplexes "outsiders." The writers understood and agreed upon its meaning immediately. Wholeness refers to several conditions in their classroom.

First, it is an attitude they hold about children. Children are treated as possessors of thoughts and feelings and particular ways of moving in the world. They are in fact fully integrated whole human beings at each moment of their lives. Successful multiage practice recognizes this truth. It takes into account children's feelings and actions as well as their thoughts. Because of this, classroom activities seem more natural, more life-like.

Second, it is a particular way the teachers plan events in their room. Even though events have a sequential minute by minute nature to them, the teachers see their parts and wholes at any moment. They have a big picture at any moment of what is going on. This would be as true for activities within a theme unit as it would be for decoding skills within the process of learning to read. Nothing really exists only for its own merit. Everything fits a larger context and is informed by a larger context. This is a characteristic that enables multiage teachers to be flexible planners. "If something doesn't get us to where we are going one way, we'll go your way." The frequent use of thematic learning and project work by the writers is justified because in the children's minds, the unit makes up a whole, a whole that has meaning for them.

Third, wholeness is also used to describe situations in their stories where past events are linked to present events or home and school became linked through the work of a child. They know their school world is tied to the child's home world. Because this is such an essential element to successful multiage environments, the writers give it a category of its own.

7. The Teacher Understands and Promotes Continuity. The writers see continuity as a major characteristic of multiage settings, especially those settings where children remain in one classroom for more than one year or with a team for a series of years. Fundamentally, continuity describes a condition of connection for a child with past learnings and events in his or her life. Thus, continuity could represent people together over time, content learned within a theme or unit, time spent in prolonged study, common activities and values between home and school, and the child's realization of membership in a group for a period of time. With continuity, the child knows his or her school setting with familiarity and the child is known with familiarity. It allows teachers to "really know a child in all ways." It allows the child time to grow in normal ways—spurts and plateaus. It also recognizes the importance of a predictable group for the child.

"'Real learning' has a quality of personal confirmation for the learner."

8. The Teacher Promotes a Community of Learners. Learning in a multiage environment is process as well as product oriented. The focus is as much on the "doing" as the "done." Children are expected to err as a natural part of their learning. If error is ridiculed, the environment will be unsafe for children's educational health. The writers agree that successful multiage practice requires the teacher promote a feeling of community in the classroom. Their writings evidence this powerfully. Community is taught and modeled. Children are taught how to help each other and how to ask for help. They solve group problems together. They share their successes and failures together. A sense of group is fostered in order that diversity becomes appreciated for what it is and so that diversity can be used in the learning process. Friendship, cooperation, and self-esteem are all fostered by these intentional community settings. In order for all these things to occur, the learning that occurs in the multiage classroom must be appropriate.

9. The Teacher Promotes Active Learning. Children and adults learn by doing but for children it is the predominant mode of constructing what they know about the world. All learning of course has mental involvement. Successful multiage activities promote a participation that is beyond the mental. Children engage the concrete realities of their world. They measure it, plant it, dig in it, stack it, build it, draw it, cook it. Mixed-ability groupings require active learning because it creates so many different models for children to choose or to get help from. These activities are high interest work and the variety of ages serve to push the pace of the learning. Children see others doing what they cannot yet do but know they must. A learning community is a safe place to be. You can practice what you do before you have to do it. The Collaborative understands this essential property of multiage settings.

10. The Teacher Values Different Kinds of Learning. They know how to organize their settings to take advantage of active learning activities. They acknowledge that learning is sometimes "in the air" in their classrooms and they promote that condition by "priming the pump" and watching the eavesdropping that occurs. They know children have different ways of acquiring knowledge and that authentic learning is a lengthy and ongoing process of interaction with people and things in the school environment. Critical to the interactions is the necessity to talk about what is being learned. They know that classroom interaction without verbal processing is both intellectually sterile and open to misunderstanding. They also seem to know that the manifestation of intelligence takes many forms beyond the verbal and they honor and support the activities that promote these manifestations. Explore Time, a highly valued scheduled period for each teacher, is a time when these distinct ways of coming to know each other and the immediate world are able to flourish.

11. The Teacher Promotes Conversation. The teachers know that if activity is the mode of learning, then talk is the mediator between the internal dialogue and the external representation of that dialogue — the spoken evidence that something has been learned. They also know that our knowledge is modified through our social discourse with other learners. Conversation seems to be the main ingredient for everything that goes on in their rooms. Children, surrounded by language, learn to use it and in multiage settings, the models are such that learning to talk about learning is promoted. Language and talk become the connector between teacher, student, object, and thought. The writers believe that rooms forever quiet are dangerous places.

The stories from which these characteristics emerged comprise the next section of the report and include a referencing of characteristics with each story. We also reference more conventional daily classroom events thinking this would enable teachers to find how the writers handled these parts of a conventional classroom day.

> *"Conversation seems to be the main ingredient for everything that goes on in their rooms."*

Chapter 7

Anne Bingham

Shelburne Village School
Shelburne, Vermont

Snapshots of a Multiage Community

"Why would you want to teach several grades together?" The daughter of a friend has just found out what I do. She is mystified. Her tone of voice says, "Why in the world do you do this?"

I ponder briefly. How to condense into a few sentences all the many reasons for my uncommon choice of a teaching setting? I say: "You know it's really much more natural. Families and neighborhoods have mixed ages. It's only in schools that people are segregated by age."

Another day I might have said: "The children learn from each other. They see models of behavior, or skills they will learn next. They help each other."

Actually, the beliefs which undergird my multiage choice are so complex, one answer cannot suffice. Many of those beliefs are shared with my more traditional teacher friends. Yet I feel, somehow, that I can act on them more effectively when children of different ages are learning together. Although I constantly examine, criticize, and revise my classroom learning environment, I cannot imagine teaching without at least a two grade-level range interacting around me.

Let me begin by recording some pictures, snapshots, of how my own multiage class looks in action. Currently I am teaching four grade levels, kindergarten through grade three. The kindergartners are in school for a half-day only. In the afternoon I have first through third grades. The first pictures include all grade levels, working on a similar assigned task, most individually.

Writing and Learning Together

It is Monday morning. Out come our journals. We talk first in a group about the weekend. What has happened since we last saw each other? What events from the past week might we record in our journals? I am priming the pump, helping children plan before they face the empty page. Then we get to work; five, six, seven, and eight year olds writing together.

Mark is busy drawing a page full of puppies. He has been reporting daily on his family's search for a new puppy. Mark, a second grader, is still more comfortable drawing first in preparation for what he will say when he writes. Some children his age write first and then illustrate. The youngest children in our group, five and six year olds, draw and then write about the picture. Jerry is drawing his new T-shirt and sunglasses, Mary Lou has a page full of balloons, and Cindy, a birthday cake. Both girls attended the same birthday party yesterday. Stephanie, who is five, draws herself and her brothers letting their baby snapping turtle go in a pond. Then she writes: "RAYMOND JOHN AND ME LET R TRL GO."

Scattered about among the illustrators, are other children busy getting narrative down on paper. Laurie needs to rehearse, in conversation with me, a story about falling into a stream while trying to catch a frog. She giggles a lot. The story is funny and will be one of her better journal entries this year. I leave her and move on. Alan is writing about a movie, but takes time to help Jimmy spell a word. Betsy's piece is about some seals she saw on a recent trip to California. She and Susie collaborate a bit on their topics, rehearsing what they will put down on the page. Susie is recording the remodeling of her home. These children are mostly seven and eight years old.

There are plenty of good models here for the beginning writers. I also encourage children to help and support each other through questions and through conversation about their writing as well. How do they learn to do this? I talk from time to time about where children can look for help. We discuss helping each other. They know this is an accepted activity. I continuously model for them ways of helping, especially in our whole group sharing, when writing is read aloud and discussed.

Ray is staring at an empty page, so when Laurie and I finish talking I head his way. He may be stuck on what to write today or he may simply need to talk about his information and decide where to begin.

Jimmy's mother helps me on Monday mornings. I really needed her at the beginning of the year. For a while most of my four kindergartners and six first graders were dictating stories. Her presence enabled me to circulate. I could encourage older writers or talk with students about their topics to help get the writing started.

Now that many families need two incomes, it is harder to find classroom volunteers. Jimmy's mother has her own business, but she takes Mondays off and generously donates an hour of this time to us each week. It is much appreciated. Dependable parent help not only benefits me, but brings family and school together in a meaningful way.

Now we can both circulate and chat with children about their topic for the day. We give spelling assistance when asked, and either one of us may sit with the youngest children when they are ready to write.

These new writers are starting to write with "kid spelling," as I term "invented spelling." They need lots of support as this process begins. Soon they will be more independent. They will also extend their time with the journals. Just now they tend to finish first. The routine is to show me their work and read it to me before putting the journal away. Then there is a group of manipulatives which they may use and space on the rug for quiet exploration. Others continue writing and illustrating.

Later some children volunteer to share their journals orally with the group. Times of coming together as a class family, both before and after an activity like writing, have an important function. Before coming to our journals, we shared a prewriting/planning process which can later be internalized by children. After writing we make public our work and refine it together.

First graders, with two or three sentences, are as likely to volunteer in that circle as Laurie, a third grader, with her frog story.

Students may point out strengths in a piece of writing, as when Jody reads a story about his cat.

"It reminds me of my dog."

"I liked the part where you say how it feels when she sleeps on your bed, 'She keeps my feet warm.'"

Carla reads, "I like horseback riding. It is fun. I got bucked off. Then I went to the hospital."

The children are full of questions. They want her to include more information: "Does your horse usually buck? Why did she do it this time? Were you scared? How were you hurt?"

Here is where I model and structure ways children may help each other: the importance of finding something positive to comment about, questions pointing to information that might have been left out or parts of a story that don't make sense, or conversation that might expand the writing.

In this sharing circle children come to accept the work of each classmate, supporting the efforts of younger, less experienced children along with older writers, enjoying what each has to offer.

This is a multiage classroom in action. Now let's open the door on another day, for a different snapshot.

"There are plenty of good models here for the beginning writers."

Graphing Experiences: Following the children's lead

Yesterday we had a cheese tasting in our room, part of a food study theme. The children had nibbled cubes of cheese stuck on colored toothpicks: green toothpicks held Swiss cheese; yellow, mozzarella; red, cheddar. The children didn't know what kinds I'd given them, and they voted for their favorite by dropping one toothpick in a basket.

Today we are going to graph the results. I have the colored toothpicks glued on a paper and some printed labels nearby: "ROOM A CHEESE TASTING," "SWISS," "MOZZARELLA," "CHEDDAR." Yesterday we had already discussed in general some ways to record the results of our experience, and the children had asked for plain paper, lined paper, and graph paper. All of these are now available, and the children set to work, each in their own way, to record and label. Toothpicks are represented by lines, dots, bars, or squares, horizontally or vertically. Bars might be labeled or a color key provided. Again five through eight year olds all carry out the assignment together.

The older children tend to make traditional bar graphs, probably because this year and last year they had already had graphing experiences and carried pictures of graphs in their heads. These were the children who had asked for graph paper.

Jay, age six, asks me for toothpicks, any color, shoves ten together and draws around them in a block. He colors the block yellow. That represents mozzarella. Then he does the same thing with seven toothpicks (cheddar) and three (Swiss), coloring each block appropriately.

Lindy, age five, revises the results so that cheddar "wins." This seems perfectly appropriate to her, as cheddar is her favorite.

The variety of their representations reflect both the children's individuality and also their diversity of development and experience.

This graphing activity was part of a thread of experiences with representation which ran through the year. Some took place in the afternoon, when our kindergartners had gone home, others in the morning when all were present. Activities included recording the colors of cars which passed the school in ten minutes one day, and counting letters of the alphabet used in newspaper headlines on another day. Both of these activities involved first tallying and then representing the results on a graph.

After the latter activity, Mandy and Susie (ages seven and eight) were inspired to use Explore Time to collaborate on a graph showing the distribution of first letters in the first names of all the children in the four multiage classrooms in our school, eighty-three children. Explore Time is a free choice period when many different activities go on simultaneously. My job in that case was to provide them with the requested class lists, alphabet tally sheets, and graph paper. They

"Dependable parent help not only benefits me, but brings family and school together in a meaningful way."

made the selection of inch graph paper after I had offered some options. This project was entirely their own idea.

For the first time this year I extended the graphing experience beyond bar graphs. The children were enthusiastic leading me to ask myself, "Why limit this? Is there something that says primary children can only handle bar graphs?"

So we did a line graph every morning as we took the lunch count, recording each day how many children had ordered hot lunch. At the end of one week we could see which lunch had been chosen by the most children: the ever popular hot dog!

There was room on the paper for seven more days, so the next week we represented the number of lunches ordered in one color and orders of milk in another. At the end of that week Mandy had a request and a prediction, "Let's do it for two more days. The third graders are going on a trip Tuesday so there won't be as many hot lunches. Maybe the milk line will meet the lunch line on our graph." She was right, it did. Older children or children with special talents push the class to new levels of thinking, one of the many advantages of diversity. Mandy was frequently our model for moving beyond the immediate question and extending our thinking in creative ways.

Our last graph of the year, a circle graph, came four days before school was out. One of the multiage traditions in our schools is "Stuffed Animal Day" when each child (and teacher) brings a favorite stuffed animal to school. We made a list of our visitors that day: four bears, three tigers, one parrot, one penguin, two bunnies, etc. I had twenty children in my class so had drawn a circle divided into twenty equal parts. Each child had a copy of this, and working from our list, sometimes in partners to help one another, readers paired with non-readers, they colored in the segments of the circle. The individual selected a color or a pattern (red polka dots, purple stripes) for each animal and colored the appropriate number of circle segments. Some children had time to label or make a key for their graph.

These pictures are snapshots of the whole class in action, individuals working alone, or a few children working together. The learning is supported by having models and helpers among the children and by the experience of being models and helpers. Learning is also supported by talk among the children as they work out problems together or react to one another's work. The natural diversity of life as it is seen outside the classroom is cherished and valued within.

"The natural diversity of life as it is seen outside the classroom is cherished and valued within."

The Individual in a Diverse Classroom

Every classroom is diverse. Every classroom is multi-level. All teachers must be aware of differences in their students' reading level, development, learning style, interests, sociability, and home life, just to name a few factors. So why stretch the age-level difference to compound this already existing problem for teachers? Because it doesn't compound the problem. Instead, in a number of ways, it leads to solutions.

A wider age range solves the problem of meeting individual needs in ways which reflect the learning that takes place out of school in families, extended families, and neighborhoods: learning by watching, learning by eavesdropping, learning by sharing and interacting, learning by talking together. Mary Lou's observation of three older children provides a good example:

Learning Models

Mandy, Susie, and June, second and third graders, had become very involved in word puzzles. Their excitement with this activity was palpable. They'd completed several puzzles I'd given them related to a study of food and nutrition, and now, during Explore Time, were asking for more. I found a "word find" in my file that lacked an accompanying word list. "This looks hard. Would you three like to help me find the words and create a list? I think it's all about dairy products."

They were eager for the challenge, so I made copies for each, and with unmistakable excitement they began. Working together and checking frequently with me they developed a long list of words from "ice cream" and "yogurt" to "condensed milk."

During all this time there was a silent, fourth member of the group whom I observed with interest. Mary Lou, a first grader, was sitting at the same table very close to the others, coloring a dot-to-dot cow. As she produced a fine black and white Holstein, complete with bright pink udder and surrounded by large yellow raindrops, she watched intently and listened. I don't think she said a word, but was in the midst of this word find excitement for forty minutes. Her eyes constantly flitted between her picture and the others. She was obviously engaged, participating vicariously in an activity which she can look forward to participating in before long. She also saw that the tools of reading, with which she was currently struggling, could be used in a playful context in addition to reading stories. What a model she had of excitement over reading, words and their meaning!

On another occasion Susie came to me with a story she'd written which held a surprise for me. It was full of conversation all properly surrounded by quotation marks, something she had not done before. Susie had been listening to me carefully go over rules for quotation marks with another child who had a story with much conversation. She had learned by eavesdropping.

Frequently when I start working with an individual or small group on regrouping in math, I will find that the work goes smoothly because of eavesdrop learning. The concept has already been introduced, without my realizing it, because the child has listened while I worked with another student.

Watching and listening can often seem like the child is "just hanging out." It looks like passive, dependent behavior. Later when the child produces something unexpected, I realize that it was a needed period of preparation, an active watching and an active listening. It is the teacher's job to observe and decide how long to let this passive seeming behavior continue, realizing that the watching and listening are all a part of learning.

Responding to Student Needs

This is not to suggest that I have no curriculum, no plans. Obviously I make plans to teach regrouping and am prepared to respond to a child's readiness for information on quotation marks. multiage teachers must plan constantly, both for the group and for individual learning, as well as be alert to children's own rhythms of learning from one another.

As a multiage teacher I can never put a child into a slot labeled "second grade" and simply lay out second-grade expectations. A good teacher wouldn't do that anyway. The wide developmental range not only forces me to individualize learning, but provides tools to respond by giving me experience with a longer stretch of academic continuum and a wider range of development. When an unusual first grader demonstrates readiness to learn regrouping in math, I am prepared through my experience with the second and third grade math curriculum.

Meeting all these needs requires a variety of approaches: children working alone as with math practice or quiet reading; children working in partners, same or different age; children working in small groups, different ages together for many projects, same level for learning specific academic skills; and everybody together as we begin a new activity, share our projects and have a daily story and discussion. I'm still surprised at how well the diverse group can operate as we all work on similar projects with individual students functioning at their own level, as with the journal writing and the graphing activities. The classroom becomes a workshop.

My role in the workshop is one of moving about and talking to children, helping them stretch what they do to greater lengths or depths, supporting the process. Perhaps I am oiling the machinery to keep it running. A metaphor I like better is that of tending a garden: feeding, watering, cultivating, even weeding.

"A workshop is student-centered (supporting the) individuals' rigorous pursuit of their own ideas," writes Nancie Atwell, in her book *In the Middle*. In the primary years this process needs lot of support and adult direction.

The workshop model provides direction to individuals while giving students a sense of ownership in their work. In my classroom during a language arts block, Laurie may choose to complete a picture in her journal, while Mary Lou selects some handwriting practice, and Alan reads. Most of the time children choose their own topics for writing, books for quiet reading, manipulative materials to assist them with math practice. Within this freedom, each child knows my expectations.

This brings us to a big assumption needed by multiage teachers, by anyone who individualizes student work successfully: an under girding belief in the learners as active and capable. It is necessary to step in and guide children in school. It is equally necessary to let go and trust, as when I talked to Laurie about her frog story and then walked away to give her time to write, or allowed Susie and Betsy to talk together about their journal entries.

During Explore Time the child's ownership of learning is primary. One day this spring I happened to look over a shelf separating our "coat room" from the rest of the classroom. There was five-year-old Lindy sprawled in her own little world, making an animal book. She had created a workspace for herself on the floor and was carefully drawing, surrounded by everything she might need: a book of animal pictures, baskets of crayons and markers, scotch tape, and an assortment of paper.

When to push or pull, when to direct, when to wait, watch, and let go. These are difficult decisions. I set the scene, provide the materials; then I must trust that learning can take place without my direct involvement at every moment. Within the diversity of learners in our multiage family, there are many teachers as well.

> *"During Explore Time the child's ownership of learning is primary."*

Learning Theory: Spider Webs and a Time to Explore

• continuity
• holistic view of learning
• Explore Time
• active learning
• open-ended time
• community of learners
• reading
• mathematics

When I was a graduate student at the University of Vermont, Lyman Hunt, one of my professors, used to show a couple of slides each year. These were his metaphors for two different views of learning. One picture was a railroad track, the other a spider web.

The railroad track represents learning that is totally sequential, step by step. Each step must be taken before the next can be attempted. Nothing can be skipped. Some things, in fact, must be learned this way. Schools have generally been good at providing for this kind of learning.

The spider web represents a more holistic model. Learning like this can be tangential, skipping sideways on the spider web. There is room for the unexpected, for surprises, for the sudden insight. It is possible, too, to slide back and pick up missed bits or to leap forward. So much learning is like this; we need to provide for it in schools as well.

Much language learning, for example, is non-sequential. Children speak words before they fully understand their meaning or can accurately pronounce them. They keep trying and conversing and listening, picking up information from varied sources. There are parallels in learning to read and write as well.

In a multiage classroom, as in the world outside of school, children are surrounded by many levels and kinds of activity. Mary Lou sees reading happening as the older girls play a word game. She hears Laurie read her frog story and watches Adam's efforts to write in cursive. They, in turn, become her teachers, and as they help her they reinforce what they know and where they have been. It is a complex web of opportunity.

During the last week of school some children dragged out the dishpan full of Unifix cubes and started stringing them across the classroom. I saw this out of the corner of my eye while helping others finish up a weaving project. It seemed to be the younger ones, fives and sixes. Then I noticed some seven year olds involved too.

"Do they really need to be doing this?" I asked myself. "It seems they've done this many times before." But it was the last week of school and I was busy. I let it go.

Fifteen minutes later I looked up to see Mark and Casey making their way, hands and knees, along the train of cubes. Mark carrying a clipboard, was looking very official. Every time Casey counted and removed ten cubes, Mark made a line on his paper. I joined them to see that Mark was tallying in fives 卌. "Where did he learn this?" I wondered. "Oh yes, the tallying we did last month in our graphing project, counting letters in headlines."

Mark counted his sets of five, two at a time, to find hundreds, since each line represented ten. I suggested he circle these groups (卌 卌). He didn't really need me, but found this a help in keeping track. When they finished we posted their tally sheet with a sign:

IT TAKES 453 UNIFIX CUBES TO GO ACROSS ROOM A.
CASEY
MARK R.

"Now," Casey said. "Let's see how long the room is the other way."

Moving sideways on the spider web, the boys had applied all they knew about tens, ones, and hundreds. They had used tallying skills learned on earlier class projects. They had also observed me, when we played "Twenty Questions," tallying the questions in fives. This particular project, however, was their own and they were motivated enough to stick with it for almost an hour. Synthesis is another way to describe what they had done, as they combined what they knew about numeration and tallying to complete this project.

This kind of learning happens when a continuity of experience builds, when children are allowed to mess about creatively exploring materials, and when second graders are allowed to do "kindergarten things" and kindergartners are given an opportunity to watch and participate.

Parallel to their learning is mine. Just when I question Mark and Casey's choice of an Explore Time activity, they pull everything together and excite me with their application and extension of knowledge. They teach me once again to trust them with their learning.

Just when I wonder about Jay and Jimmy's days on end in the block area, they come to me for help in measuring a structure or writing a sign. Or a visiting math teacher says, "I can see your children have done work with spatial relations. It shows."

In *In the Middle* by Nancie Atwell, Donald Graves says: "It is entirely possible to read about children, review research and text-books. . . yet still be completely unaware of their processes of learning. . . Unless we actually structure our environments to free our-selves for effective observation and participation. . . we are doomed to repeat the same teaching mistakes again and again?" Although he refers specifically to the teaching of writing, I believe what he states is broadly applicable.

Value of Explore Time

Our Explore Time provides that ideal time to observe because the agenda is usually the children's, not mine. Sometimes I am intensely involved hearing a group of children. At other times I can allow myself to observe. I come to know individual students, their interests, and learning styles better.

Explore Time is also one way to add an element of choice and responsibility to each day. With the choice of an activity, materials and companions, comes the responsibility for completion, clean-up, and cooperation.

The same concrete materials needed in other primary classrooms are needed in multiage rooms: materials for arts and crafts, including various art media and assorted sizes and types of paper, games, books, computers, and math manipulatives. Most of these manipulatives, such as Unifix Cubes, Pattern Blocks. Cuisenaire Rods and Tangrams, challenge children at many levels. Along with this diversity of materials, multiage children need sufficient time to investigate them, to explore.

The result of the exploration is that when I decide Cuisenaire Rods, for example, will be a useful way to introduce or enhance some math concept, the children are already familiar with these materials and their inherent structure. They have had ample time to play with them and discover that structure for themselves.

Explore Time also means that a third grader will have blocks available for the fun of constructing an elaborate castle or to use in a spatially-oriented project such as inventing a village or playground. Third-grade rooms often do not have blocks. First graders, on the other hand, may observe and be introduced to activities that would not ordinarily be found in a first-grade classroom.

I have used a board game called "Bionic Bullfrog" with some older children working on multiplication facts. Included with the game is a table to check those facts as needed. Ray taught the game to Jimmy, a first grader. Jimmy latched onto the game as his favorite and played it with anyone he could get to join him, teaching many of the younger children. Was Jimmy moving ahead on the spider web?

Children in multiage classrooms teach others all the time. They may learn from one another how to play a game, to use the computer, to clean up the room, to borrow lunch money from the office, to solve problems, to write their name in cursive, even to tie shoes. They provide models as Mandy, Susie, and June did while playing word games. They model routines for taking lunch count and attendance, or picking up after Explore Time. They teach directly as Ray did when Jimmy learned to play "Bionic Bullfrog."

They also help the teacher as Adam did one day during Explore Time.

Betsy, Mark and I were on the rug working with Unifix Cubes, learning to carry two-digit numbers. There was a lot going on: block building in one corner, two children with earphones at the tape recorder, board games, drawing, a parent working with two

"They teach me once again to trust them with their learning."

children at the computer. One group of younger children, mostly kindergartners, was at a nearby table creating constructions with a set of cubes that fit together in various ways. The noise level was fairly high and their voices got louder and louder. I spoke to them rather sharply, and things quieted down. The atmosphere remained calmer, but I didn't particularly note this because I was so engaged in helping Mark and Betsy. Later when I stopped to talk with the little group at the table, Ryan volunteered, "Adam helped us." He seemed pleased.

"He helped you with your construction?" I asked.

"No, but he helped us."

Further questioning clarified Mike's assertion, as Adam, a third grader, joined the group. Adam had realized that the children were squabbling about the construction cube because some had a good many more than others. The set is small. He had come from his game to help the younger children divide the cubes evenly.

The construction crew seemed happy with the result, Adam was pleased, and I was delighted: The younger ones had not only been assisted in solving their problem, they had been shown a model for problem solving by another child. They had experienced the solution of a problem among peers, without the intervention of an adult. Adam had quietly taken over a piece of classroom management, imperceptibly, as I continued to work elsewhere. I might have been unaware of the whole sequence had it not been for Mike's comment, "Adam helped us."

Explore Time is a significant part of each day. The stories about Mark and Casey, Ray and Jimmy, Adam and Mike all happened during Explore Time. They happened because during that time children can frequently explore materials in their own way, because there is time for children to watch and to be both teachers and learners, because they are surrounded by many levels and varieties of activity. Explore Time allows the spider web to function.

"Children in multiage classrooms teach others all the time."

Together Over Time: The Gift of Continuity

One of the things that creates a community or defines a family is a common history and culture. When people are together over time they not only know each other better, but have a wealth of shared experience, a common memory, and often a set of traditions.

In multiage classrooms the children usually stay for two or three years in the same setting. Each year there are some changes in the family group, but overlapping members convey the common memory. In our school four multiage classes make up a program sharing many traditions. Siblings may come in expecting traditions their brothers and sisters have remembered, for they already consider themselves part of the community. This legacy contributes to the school memories our "graduates" take with them.

Our day camp is like that, an all-day spring outing held every year for all four multiage classes. Recently while shopping at a local bagel bakery I met a former student, now in college. "Do you still have day camp?" she wanted to know, and "singalong" and "Friday morning special?"

The following story is one of community development. It is the kind of happening that could not have occurred without the wider range of age and experience that are a part of multiage.

Developing Community and a Shared History

Jay brought a sprouted maple seed in from recess. He and Ethan had been gathering handfuls of these seeds daily (helicopters, they called them), and I had provided them with small waxed paper bags to carry the seeds home. Jay reported planting them in several pots at his house. This new seed had been gently removed from the ground for it had already sprouted two tiny leaves. "It wouldn't have survived in the spot I found it," Jay explained. I found a paper cup and some soil for his baby tree, and he brought it to our class circle on the rug to share with the group.

The ensuing conversation led Sam to ask, "Why did they cut down that big maple tree?" Sam is a third grader, Jay is in first grade. What is a big stump on the playground used to be a huge maple tree. Jay can't remember this tree, but Sam can.

In the conversation which followed, totally unplanned by me, the older children wove Jay's seedling into a tapestry of remembrances, drawing the younger children into the common history of the school and the class.

They said: "You know how you say to a friend, 'Meet you at the big stump at recess?' We used to say, 'Meet you at the big tree,'" and they expressed, too, how much they missed the big tree and what it had meant to them as a special playground landmark. Every spring the tree had been tapped and a bucket hung to gather the sweet sap.

The tree had been cut down because it was sick and dying due partly to the soil compacted because of years of children's feet running and playing over its roots. The oldest children could even remember the year a fence had been put around the tree in an effort to save it.

The conversation meandered a bit, as such talk often does. One child wondered whether there had once been a woods, lots of trees, where the school now stands. Someone else said, "No, because if there had been a woods we would see lots of stumps." There was speculation about the digging out or decomposition of stumps over time.

Mandy, another third grader, said she'd heard that the school was one of the oldest buildings in town. She went on to tell about the library across the street, which had been a store, then a priest's house, then a store again before it became the library.

The older children drew Jay and the younger ones into the common history of the class and extended their participation in this community beyond the bounds of their short years in school.

Such experiences contribute a powerful force toward developing a sense of family, in which the children will acquire a feeling of responsibility for one another. Such a family can learn to work together. Cooperative activity, support for one another, and a sense of belonging can be outcomes when a group of children have been together over time.

Developing Trust and a Sense of Family

When a child stays with the same teacher for two or three years, teachers, children, and families also come to know each other better. Communication is easier and there is less time required to get started in the fall.

Carrie will especially benefit from this. Her life outside of school has not had much stability:

"I've had three fathers really," she said one day, trying to answer another child's question: "What's a stepfather."

"There was my real father, the one who made me. I never really knew him. Then the man my mother lived with for a while. I felt like he was my real father, but he was my stepfather. Then the man my mother married last summer. He's my stepfather now."

One morning Carrie brought a big teddy bear to school. "Do you know," she bragged to me, "This bear is over thirty years old?"

"Was it your mother's bear?" I asked.

"No, my bionic, biolic, biogic—oh, I don't know the word!"

"Biologic," I offered. "That's it," she said triumphantly. "It was my biologic father's," and she took off across the room to show the bear to a friend.

As the children gradually arrive in the classroom, brief moments of conversation are possible. They chat, I chat, until the last bus arrives and we gather on the rug for the routines of attendance, lunch count, and sharing.

Almost daily Carrie stopped to see me first, to bring me updates on her mother's remarriage and pregnancy, to comment uneasily about her new stepfather. A few moments of conversation with me each morning and she was off to greet her friends. She often returned to these topics in her writing, as when she recorded the day her mother lost the baby.

With all the changes in her life one thing will remain stable for another year. Carrie's classroom and teacher will not change.

Teachers are seeing more and more children like Carrie. Significant adults in their lives live separately, and sometimes one of them drops out altogether. New relationships with stepparents are forged. These may include new brothers, sisters, aunts, uncles and grandparents. A child's life may be divided between two families whose demands and life-styles differ.

In families not disrupted by separation, both parents often work. This may mean some sort of day care after school. It sometimes means children get themselves off in the morning or arrive home before parents.

Providing a stable community in school can be very important.

When I have known a child for a year already, I can also pick up much more quickly on academics in the fall. Abby is a slow starting second grader who's reading progress has been shaky this year. When she arrives in third grade I will already know much about her strengths and weaknesses. I will know what kind of books she likes. I will know some needs and gaps in her learning that will need immediate attention. Most important, in September Abby and I will be comfortable with each other from the beginning.

August anxiety, about a new class or teacher, can be a problem for some children, especially those who form relationships with difficulty. With such children it is positive to build on the trust developed over one academic year, continuing the relationship for another.

One day after school last spring, a parent dropped by to pick up something her son had forgotten. Trailing along was Catherine, age three. I had had Bobby for two years, and in that time had watched Catherine grow. She and I had talked on just such informal occasions as this. As her mother and I conversed, Catherine wandered about the room. Suddenly she came running toward me, pink-sleeved arms stretched up, the universal child gesture asking

"Such experiences contribute a powerful force toward developing a sense of family . . ."

for a hug. How great that Catherine was already so comfortable with the setting and at least one of the people who will be a part of her schooling in a few years. She was already a member of our community. I'm sure this happens in small schools, but ours is not a small school.

To begin to trust and know one another takes time; to become a community does too. The potential for this is increased in a class to which children return for more than one year or in a cluster of such classes, an extended family within a school.

> *"To begin to trust and know one another takes time; to become a community does too."*

A Multiage Team: Pooling Our Strengths

- *teaming*
- *interaction*
- *traditions of the unit*
- *teacher as learner*
- *continuity*
- *learning community*

I heard peals of laughter, followed by loud talk and giggles as I headed for the door of Room C and a Multiage team meeting. How could anyone imagine that an important task was taking place, I wondered, by overhearing our team "working" together? Yet this pervasive laughter is characteristic of our serious work. The four of us, after teaching together for eighteen, seventeen, and ten years respectively, have become good friends with a host of happy and painful recollections. The fact that we've stayed together this long means that we have a good working relationship.

In my school there are four multiage and a number of single-grade classrooms. The Multiage teachers form a team. With four heads working together, our program has developed varied kinds of activities which would not have been possible for any one of us working alone. Although my stories thus far have been mostly about children, this one is first of all about adults and what we can accomplish working together in schools.

Sharing Interests and Strengths

For many, teaching can be a lonely occupation in which a teacher shuts the classroom door each morning and spends the day with children. Adult interaction and companionship can be painfully missing. Not so with a teaching team.

When I talk to teachers who have decided to work together as a team, they are usually enthusiastic about the process. They feel that two or three teachers, with differing personalities, interests and strengths can offer a richly varied program. Teachers can be resources for one another when a problem arises. These teams are also positive about the professional advantages of teaming, saying that the interaction stimulates professional growth.

The team concept has some advantages for children too.

Jimmy came to me at the beginning of Explore Time, "May I float?"

"Where do you think you might float? Do you have a plan?"

"I'm going to room B. Mrs. Johnson said Mike and I should try to finish our toothpick sculptures today."

"Floating" is our in-house term for going to another multiage room to choose an activity, an option during Explore Time, about forty minutes each day. One room has a piano, which children may play certain days during the week. Other rooms have sand and a reading loft. My own room offers a large block area. In addition to giving children an opportunity to choose an activity or materials not available in their own room, this can be a time to take advantage of the talents or interests of another teacher.

Liz Farman plays the piano and knows music and songs better than the rest of us. Marilyn Johnson does a beautiful job with art media and also has broad math interests. Phyllis Murray is a fine craftsperson, who has at times had sewing projects in her room, and often guides the children in craft work from yarn to paper folding.

Then there are specific materials and activities provided in different rooms each year. Marilyn finds work with structures fascinating and always has toothpick sculptures available in her room each fall. I get out batteries, bulbs, and small electric motors during the winter months, and for a while that is a big attraction in my room. Science is a fascinating area for me.

Most important to the children, floating during Explore Time gives them a chance to work with friends in one of our three other multiage classes. It provides time with an "extended family" or community beyond their own classroom.

Planning Special Events

Our teacher team works together in other ways. In addition to Explore Time, much field trip planning is done jointly. Every Friday afternoon we gather for a sing-a-long. On Friday mornings we have another kind of shared time, known as "Friday morning special."

Friday morning special is an activity planned to take second and third graders a step beyond Explore Time. First graders are occupied with another activity at this time. Children sign up for a single "special" in one room. Usually there are four sign-up slots for children from my room in each other room, so my students go in several different directions. There is a reason for this; later they must plan to share what they have learned with the rest of the class. The children who have gone together to one special plan a presentation. They convey information, teach games, and plan demonstrations. They develop the skill of communicating an experience to the rest of the group.

Many Friday morning special activities are science experiments or games of logical thinking, but such topics as language games or drama are also included from time to time. Some of my titles during the last year were "Crackle, Buzz, Zap" (static electricity), "Castle Building" (directing another person to place blocks spatially), "Flicker, Flicker" (science experiments with a candle), and "Mime Time" (pantomime).

Together we also developed a further extension of our daily program for third graders. As they seemed to need something extra, we planned a series of mini-courses, pulling together all third graders from the four classrooms. They spend several weeks during the year with our school counselor, have a first aid class with the nurse, and book discussion groups led by parents. At times one member of the team has taught a short mini-course. This group produced a newspaper one year, a collection of poetry another.

Teaming also provides built-in consultation on students. In the fall, I not only have children returning to my classroom from the year before, but those who have been in one of our other multiage rooms. I have come to know these children through our joint team activities. If I am unsure about a child's academic strengths or the best choice of materials for a new student, I can walk across the hall and ask another teacher. The ease with which we confer about children is a real plus.

Once or twice during the year we study a theme together. One day last December the children and I sat spellbound while another class presented "The Riddle of the Drum," a Mexican fairy tale. Cardboard puppet animals, a king and a princess bounced along the edge of an overturned table, used as a stage. My class had been studying Mexico as well, but had not heard this amusing story. The puppet show was part of a sharing time planned to culminate the theme "North American Neighbors," about which our four multiage classroom had been studying simultaneously. This room was filled with exhibits of Mexican artifacts and with pinatas the children had made. Our own classroom had similar exhibits. Preceding the puppet show, we had made our presentation, "A Mexican ABC."

After the puppet show, the entire audience picked up and moved to another room, and then still another, where we watched enactments of Canadian Inuit folk tales. Mexican and Canadian flags hung in the hall connecting our four classrooms. There, the day before, we had all shared in a "Good Neighbor Snack" for which our class had provided tropical fruits, hicama slices, and nachos. The opportunity for sharing of learning information on "North American Neighbors" was a direct outgrowth of team planning and made the study more meaningful to the children.

In June we join together in an all day outing known as "day camp." We spend the day outdoors, have a picnic supper, and return the children to waiting families in early evening. This, along with our Friday afternoon sing-a-long, has become a community tradition, the intention of which is to bring the entire extended family together.

The shared experience of the teachers with day camp goes back many more years than the children's. Each June as the day approaches, we watch the weather reports and recall to one another the rainy day when we returned to the school at 7:30 p.m. covered with mud, but to the surprise of waiting parents, with smiles as well. We remember a ferry ride under sparkling sun, a day when we all had to shelter in a lakeside dressing room during a thunderstorm, the "hike to Canada" and "the terrible year of the mosquito."

"The children . . . convey information, teach games, and plan demonstrations."

At each day camp we close a day of hiking, nature activities and outdoor play with a farewell campfire sing-a-long for our third graders. We have such good times that we no longer have to ask for help; parents regularly volunteer for this trip. Both mothers and fathers take the day off to come.

Teaming and Autonomy: Finding a Balance

Styles of teaming vary a great deal. Some teacher teams work intensively, sharing all children and all planning all the time. Others work together minimally for parts of a week or even part of the year, or they exchange children occasionally. Teachers of two grade levels even team part of each day, in order to try a multiage situation.

Our team has struck a balance so that we are able to maintain a good deal of independence within the team structure. We are each responsible for our own kindergarten through grade three class of about twenty children. Most of my day-to-day activities are with my own family group in a self-contained setting. These are the children for whom I am primarily responsible. I plan for them academically, follow their progress and report to their parents. Daily Explore Time, special Friday events, joint themes, and trips are regular departures from this and enrich the program.

It is important to us to have some autonomy in which to express our own special styles, interests, and concerns. If one member submerges this sense of self in teaming, too much energy and commitment will be lost.

In a great many ways I am what I am as a teacher because of these people with whom I have worked closely for so many years. I have laughed with them, agonized with them, cajoled them to see things my way, given in to someone else's ideas. Most of all, I have learned so much from my teammates and experienced such deep friendship with them that my teaching life has been immeasurably enriched.

"Our team has struck a balance so that we are able to maintain a good deal of independence within the team structure."

Chapter 8

Peggy Dorta

Underhill Elementary School
Underhill, Vermont

Dear Mrs. Osborne,

• valuing children's diversity
• classroom community
• reading
• teacher as learner

I really appreciate the three R's you helped me with and I remember that wonderful play we put on that year. I also loved listening as you read "Evangeline" and I learned a lot about westward expansion. I appreciate these things, even after thirty-four years have gone by.

Did you know that Gloria would make a fine horticulturist? Did you learn how to count to ten in Spanish? Did you ever see that map that Joe kept in his back pocket showing the many wonderful places he had lived? Did you realize that Jill ended up with a reading comprehension problem in junior high, but could still read faster than any of the rest of us?

You see, I have become a teacher and am still learning from the experiences I had during my life and schooling. My priorities have evolved partially from the reflections I have from my early years of being the one behind the desk.

In reflecting upon my own experiences I try to become the teacher I want to be. . . that vision!! I feel I must approach my job empowered to make sense of what I do and to encourage each individual that I come in contact with to do the same, whatever his or her circumstances may be.

Sincerely,
Peggy Rohrs Dorta

"Peggy, take Gloria out into the hall and have her read to you!"

I was in the fourth grade, an impressionable nine-year-old, with a strong desire to please and a pretty good academic background so far. Several times each week the teacher would make the same request of me. I would dutifully shuffle off into the hallway (it was dark as I recall) and head for the landing (it had the only window for light) with my chair. Gloria would follow with a book, her chair, and a very wide, red-lipstick smile that seemed always to be there.

The task at hand was to help Gloria decode the story in front of us. It was from a basal reader that involved Dick, Jane, Sally, and a red balloon. I knew that fourth graders should be beyond that, but that was our task.

Gloria and I had been put into a dyad as underdog and top dog. I was given the message that I was a capable student and she was reinforced as being "behind." This early experience was so one-sided. And yet, I learned something very important from that forced lesson.

After we rushed through the teacher's plan we would have time left over to talk about Gloria's favorite interest. . . plants. I learned that Gloria was very capable indeed! She knew more about growing things than anyone I had ever read or heard of. Her expression changed dramatically as she described her buds and blossoms and what she did to take care of them. I still wonder if she is the horticulturist she could be today. Did anyone ever recognize and give her the support and motivation to follow her interest and aptitude?

All Children Are Learners and Teachers

I react to that experience as I think of our multiage classroom where we all converge each day as individuals with varying ages, needs, capabilities, and interests intact. We meet in our joint learning community and share our characteristics. No one should be encouraged to believe that they are the all-around top dog and no one assigned that role of underdog. Each person brings strengths and weaknesses to be addressed. It is my job to unearth their individualism and follow through with it.

What kind of dyads do I support or offer in our multiage classroom? As I look around the room I see Sarah and Cory sitting on the couch engrossed with a book. If it's something Cory knows a lot about he may, as a so-called non-reader, be explaining the pictures to Sarah. Or Sarah may be reading about something Cory wants to learn. They may just be sharing it together.

Judd is reading his rough draft on eagles to Keith, the known expert in the class on animals. Judd may be asking advice, sharing his pride on this new found information or just conferencing.

Megan and Tony are studying the map to find where she lived in Saudi Arabia for two years. Tony has never been out of his state of Vermont and is amazed how far Megan has traveled.

Patty and Debbie have viewed cells under a microscope. Patty is quite an artist but has difficulty writing so she may be illustrating what they saw while our prolific Debbie writes captions.

A couple are sharing the computer. Two or three are working on a mural.

Children should know that they are valuable members of the group. They should believe that they are worthwhile contributors. They should expect to be teachers and learners within the classroom situation, no matter what their age, academic expression, or ability.

In my fourth grade classroom from so many years ago, Gloria sat in the last seat in the last row. The teacher's seating arrangement had to do with reading groups. The top group sat in the first row, the next highest in the second row, etc. We were also assigned seats within each row according to how fast we read when timed on our weekly oral reading sample. Jill was a speed demon and always sat in the first seat in the first row.

Joe, the son of migrant farm workers, moved in mid-year. I remember him vividly. I found him to be intriguing. He spoke only Spanish and we heard very little from him. Joe took Gloria's back seat.

His aptitude in Spanish could have allowed each of us not only to respect his language prowess, but also to learn some foreign language ourselves. The well-used map folded away in his back pocket was important to him. It was a document of the many places he had lived all over the United States. It could have been the bridge to include him into our group as a contributing, motivated member of the class, while teaching us about geography and interesting places in our country.

Kids are natural teachers. They all come with great possibilities to be tapped, nurtured, and supported. What a colossal loss if we ignore or allow ourselves to forget such resources.

Do you ever ask yourself the question "What made me the type of teacher I am?" or "Why do I emphasize what I do?" Do you reflect on what events, people, and experiences have contributed to your teaching?

In so asking, I begin to see a pattern and direction to my teaching. I become conscious of why I do what I do. I strengthen my belief that all children are learners and teachers and with time, trust, and support we all can believe in ourselves as individuals who can make a difference somehow.

"No one should be encouraged to believe that they are the all-around top dog and no one should be assigned that role of underdog."

The Circle

The circle is a tight one. All twenty-four of us fit. Knees touch, shoulders meet. We sit, anticipating class meeting. Andy has the weekly chore of class meeting leader. He sits on a special chair and declares "Are there any announcements?"

Hands fly in every direction. Andy calls on Adam to address what he is so eager to share. He seems extremely animated today as he shares his reaction to the activity we have just completed. Isak's father had whisked us all away to Botswana with his artifacts, slides, and tales of his time spent there. He had a very vivid presentation and the children had really been enthralled with it.

Class meeting. . . many teachers use circle time to offer the children an opportunity to share an object or a happening from their lives.

For me, the class meeting circle represents the cycle of learning and teaching I hope will take place in my classroom. It is a significant image, that circle. It is an emblem, a symbol.

Like so many other things that one might observe in a classroom setting, at first glance the circle may seem to be only a workable arrangement for children in order to attend. But it is so much more. It defines the parameters but not what goes on within it.

Within the meeting the children are given the opportunity to state their ideas and to explore their feelings. It is the true arena that exhibits the class cohesiveness and trust as it develops. It helps students become cognizant of the similarities and differences of their own and of others' thoughts.

The circle format is a learned one. It is important that each child be a member of the circle, not sitting behind someone, but in a position that allows him or her to see everyone else's face. We discuss how important it is to have eye contact when you communicate. In so sitting, it also reiterates the emphasis on each person belonging to the whole.

What takes place within the circle meeting depends largely on the timing of the school year and is influenced by the modeling of the veteran classmates. In September in a multiage class about half the children have the trust it takes to really express themselves without the fear of speaking out and letting what they've shared hang out there to possibly be rejected. They have a history from the year before.

By November most of the class feels at home in the group. This is when I put on my observer hat and watch for those who just don't yet feel comfortable. What do they need? Support? A question or comment to draw them in?

Signs of Growth

Michael, a first year kiddo, sat for most of the year, until about March, without saying boo within the circle meeting. Oh yes, an occasional nod of agreement or three cents worth, but nothing that he really gave of himself or about himself. I had been watching him carefully. He seemed to be involved with the group conversations and an interested, albeit passive, participant. So when he cut in one day and stated "I'm going to Texas to visit my father," I sat up and took heed. It's signposts like that which reflect the trust and level of involvement a person has to the group.

What other signs of growth and characteristics do I look for? There's one that I hope will come. I giggle to myself when it does. I raise my hand in circle and usually, early in the year, that means I get called on by the meeting leader right away. But later on, when the meeting really becomes theirs, I have to sit and sit and sit, waiting my turn. . . It is their meeting and I am not the leader. I am simply another participant.

I watch for the use of eye contact when speaking and listening as children learn to respond to each other. I listen for insights they gain through communication of an issue. I sense the hard work they do within the group as they problem solve together.

Kyle had a problem on the soccer field. Everybody seemed to be on his case about not following rules and hogging the ball. It was during a class meeting that this was resolved. After quite an intense discussion, not argument, but many "I" statements included, a child made a suggestion that was agreeable to all concerned. Why not make Kyle a referee for a week? That way he could learn the rules and see what happened in the game.

Well, with some ups and downs, it worked. Kyle felt needed and important. He actually was an extremely fair referee and gained the respect of his fellow players. After that week I received very few complaints about his play.

And what other kinds of discussions take place within this structure of a circle? It frequently begins with sometimes terse, usually concrete illustrations or objects. It goes on to more personal or informational diatribes and finally into a phase of real sharing, real expressions of thoughts, reactions, interests, worries, concerns, knowledge. . . you name it. . . it's usually covered.

Abby was a second year member of the class. She had muscular dystrophy. Her deer-like eyes sat in a face that had no muscle usage. She always held the same expression, one that looked sad or forlorn to the casual observer.

The first year with us it took her months even to talk about muscular dystrophy. But the first week of school that second year, I

"Kids are natural teachers. They all come with great possibilities to be tapped, nurtured, and supported."

was thrilled when up shot her hand during circle. She explained to the new members about the "disease that they couldn't catch." She told them why she never smiled with her mouth. "Watch my eyes," she said.

The trust and security she felt within that group meeting allowed her to share early on with the kids about her problems and to share ways she had learned to overcome them. It offered us the opportunity to talk about individual differences.

When Nicole was part of our lives in a multiage class, she communicated with sign language. Although she could hear, she could not express herself through oral language (apraxia). We all learned to sign. We used key signs during meetings and other times within class.

At the end of that school year each of us shared the most important time or activity that we would take with us. When it was her turn, Nicole put her two index fingers together and moved them in an outward circle in front of her. Her expression of a cycle seemed appropriate. Her entire sweeping motion signified the cycle of learning and sharing as she included us all within our circle meeting.

"I sense the hard work they do within the group as they problem solve together."

Explorers

What do Ben, Evan, Tristan, and Meredith have in common with Christopher Columbus, Ponce de Leon, Lewis and Clark, and Sally Ride? They are all explorers!

A dictionary definition of "explore" is as follows:

1. to travel in little known areas for the purpose of discovery;

2. to go over carefully; look into closely; examine.

Explore Time in our classroom takes place for the first forty to sixty minutes of the school day. The children's arrivals stagger over a period of time, but as soon as they get through that door they know what the routine is.

If you were to observe during this time period you might see two kids working at the computer center, a few involved with art materials, and others writing in their journals. Readers could be found on the couch or in the loft. Frequently, some people are playing a game or messing about (i.e., learning) with math manipulatives. You may watch one or two heading out to the library to research, especially after they've spent time at our trivia table. There may be an adult working with a small group of children, playing a word game or something. Other folks may be using the auto harp or building with blocks or Legos. Some children are problem solving a new challenge that has been presented or creating puzzles for the class to solve.

What am I doing? I spend a lot of Explore Time observing and just touching base informally with kids. Often you'll find me teaching/learning/playing a math game or creating in the art center. I might be on the couch talking about a book or magazine with someone. Frequently, I'm working one-on-one or with a small group with certain skills or materials. It's a wonderful opportunity to introduce a computer program or offer "enrichment" time to a few.

It's probably my favorite passage of the day. I know the kids like it too. So many activities and ideas start there. So much catching up or clarifying is achieved.

One day I walked in with my discovery of a new author. I had under my arm a few of her books. Each one held a collection of photographs depicting people around the world. One had a theme of breads, another baskets, and the third hats. There were so many different kinds of people and things in her books.

After a few days of poring through these books, the kids talked more and more about what other books this author might like to make. So I gathered some clippings from magazines of people in costumes. "What do you think about my photographs for my new books?" I asked.

91

We worked on that book together for quite a while. Four other books were made throughout the course of that year during Explore Time, beautiful books about cultures around the world with a lot of thought and research put into them. Explore Time offered us the opportunity to learn something new about something that really interested us.

Easing the Transition

Why else do we have Explore Time? Transitions are important for all of us. Think about what a child has already encountered by 8:00 a.m. Or what they need to do to give themselves needed time to adjust gears. Or what happened last night that should be processed or shared.

Jarod craved routine at school. He would walk in each morning, drop his backpack somewhere in the vicinity of the hook that was meant to catch it, and head for the Lego area. You could count on Jarod to keep that consistent routine.

Jarod's morning before school went something like this: He would get up and chow down a breakfast of his making. Depending upon which parent he lived with for the week, he would walk himself to the country store, about a half-mile away, and wait for the bus (often beating the storekeeper to his post), or down the one-quarter mile driveway. If he missed the bus he would walk the mile or so to school or return home for the day, whichever struck his fancy.

He often came in to school with red eyes or a new bruise I would have to report.

Jarod's home life did not offer him a lot of structure or consistency. . . thus the great need for it to come from somewhere.

One day our schedule needed to be rearranged. A parent who came in to sing with us each week was there early, taking the place of Explore Time first thing. I had planned to meet Jarod at the door, to help redirect and reorient his day. Unfortunately, I got caught across the room and watched from afar as he flew into the room, deposited his pack, pivoted, and stared in awe at the circle of children around the guitar player that sat between him and his Lego station.

Well, that morning must have been a tough one because Jarod fell apart. He threw a temper tantrum, crying and flailing about. Most of the day he was full of refusals as he wore a nasty frown.

The Legos during Explore Time offered him more than just a set routine. It offered him time to ease into the school day; to start slowly interacting with his peers; time to discuss the day with me, to take a glimpse at what would be coming; to use his creative instincts before dealing with the tasks that were so often difficult for him; and to accomplish something at the beginning and carry that feeling with him through the school day.

Transition time.

Explore Time.

A time to be able to wipe yesterday or this morning's slate clean and truly get on with today.

Catching up, Continuing on, Making Choices

Think about all of those important activities that you just can't seem to get to or that child you haven't had time to connect with or the others that really need time with you to start the day positively.

How about the writing Erin was working on and she just couldn't wait to get to today? Or the trouble Leslie had yesterday that you want to follow-up on? How about that group you want to check in with? Then there's Jeb who is really ready for more challenge. And Amy, she could use some suggestions for new authors and books.

Explore Time offers an opportunity to do all of these things. It also offers the students the time to practice making choices, to take responsibility and ownership of their learning.

It does take work and a plan to make Explore Time a successful time block. I start by looking up the word explore in some dictionaries with the class during our meeting time. We brainstorm and discuss where we've heard the word before. Then I explain that in our classroom it is a time to teach ourselves or practice something on our own.

For a few weeks I put activities out each morning and list them on the board. They can choose from that list what they'd like to do. We do a lot of discussing about what went on each day. We demonstrate how certain materials or activities can be used. So much informal peer tutoring goes on with the veteran classmates in our multiage sharing their expertise with a newer member.

As kids adapt and get used to this time, more flexibility can be used within the choices offered. They can choose one I've put out or one of their own. I do a lot of observing and give a lot of feedback to the children.

I usually have a selection of activities that include an art project, math manipulatives, a special display of books and/or magazines, a challenge, a program for the computer, the trivia table of interesting items, and assorted paper and booklets for writing. I set these activities up all year long, even though the number of children depending upon my choices decreases as the year progresses. There seem to be some kids who feel more comfortable with my offerings rather than making choices on their own. These kids, and the ones who seem to need fewer choices, are the ones I need to work with on how to make and follow through with their decisions.

There are times throughout the year when we need to review or even draw in the reins a little. In the past, I have occasionally used weekly charts for all or some of the students to write down what

"As kids adapt and get used to this time, more flexibility can be used within the choices offered."

93

they have done during Explore Time each day.

I take a lot of anecdotal notes during Explore Time. Yet, I have also learned not to worry too much about keeping track of what everyone is doing all of the time. Explore Time has taught me to trust kids' abilities to be curious, to be natural teachers for themselves and others, to be creative, and to complete tasks they're excited about.

The structure of Explore Time is also transferred to other areas of the school day. During the normally chaotic indoor recesses, the children's ability to find something to do and stick with it is admirable. When there is lag time or kids get down with a project and are waiting for others, they explore. When a substitute teacher is taking over, Explore Time is a safe bet.

Explorers discover things about themselves.
Explorers examine interests and gain confidence.
Explorers make important decisions every day.
Explorers feel ownership and responsibility for their learning.
Explorers practice.
Explorers can be discovering a process to become lifelong learners.

3-2-1-GO!!!

• *explaining multiage*
• *teacher as learner*
• *communication: staff and parents*
• *continuity*
• *perspective on child as learner*
• *teaming*

"What is this multiage?"

"Won't my child repeat a lot in her second year with you?"

"Why do you do it that way?"

"Is my child being retained for some reason?"

"Where's the research on this multiage teaching?"

Thus started my first year in a new position as a multiage teacher in a school that had never experienced such an approach. I had been teaching for nine years in a multiage philosophically based school, i.e., we all did it. I had before that been in open classrooms and other similar educational situations. There you have it. . . sixteen years of experience with multiage. . . and I was being asked questions I couldn't answer.

Whew! What did they want from me? How do I start to explain to them what I do? Is it really that different from other classrooms around me?

Gaining Parent and Community Support

Communication of what we do is an important aspect of teaching. Children need to know why they are doing what they're doing. Parents need to be involved and informed. Administrators need to see our accountability. The general public needs to see their tax dollars spent for "appropriate" education.

I went to my new job feeling confident, prepared, and excited for what I was planning to have happen in the classroom. But I was not ready for the rest of it. Thus I got caught off guard. I had thought about fellow teachers, parents, and what I'd say. I had some pat answers to questions. But I had been in an insular environment for so long, I could not anticipate the right questions.

Then came the biggie. Would I lead a public meeting to explain multiage? Warning lights went off in my head. Now I had some thinking to do. My gut reaction was "No thank you. Not yet. Not me as leader." But the final decision was out of my hands. There was to be an informational meeting in one week. The entire staff would be there to answer questions and show unity.

Yikes!

My reservations were deeply rooted in the fact that I was the new kid on the block, a block where the other people had lived for many years without me and my new approach. They had so many unanswered questions themselves that I was pretty sure I'd end up being the one on the spot. . . . . . Yep, I was!

Well, I made it through that meeting and collected a long list of the questions really on people's minds.

"I'd just quietly teach and meanwhile educate my kids' parents about the multiage experience."

"Will my kid get bored in her second year with you? Will she be challenged?"

"My child is pretty smart. Will the younger kids hold him back?"

"Do you cover the district curriculum so my child will be okay when she leaves your class?"

"Do you teach basics?"

"Will my child be threatened by being in a class with older kids?"

"Is my boy being retained?"

"Will the class be filled with those who need extra time in third grade?"

Now I could try to anticipate what their fears of change might be. I knew that I shouldn't and couldn't answer all of the inquiries, but I thought about each one to provide myself the needed clarity.

Next, how to inform the school public about this multiage approach? There were a few ways I had observed others in such a situation doing it. In one district the teaching staff, administrators, and parents studied the multiage philosophy for a year previous to starting it themselves. They met to share information they had discovered. They looked for research, observed in schools, and spent time questioning and talking in depth with experienced children, teachers, administrators, and parents.

In my school district time was a luxury. They had too many kids for some grades but not enough to form a whole new class at that grade level. Thus a three-four needed to be formed. They did not want to run it as split level, with third graders on one side of the room and fourth graders on the other. So they hired an experienced teacher to do it.

Developing a Plan

I decided that modeling was the key. I'd just quietly teach and meanwhile educate my kids' parents about the multiage experience. I'd share commonalties with my cohorts, a few steps at a time.

In a neighboring large district four multiage classrooms had been in existence for several years. After spending a great deal of time researching multiage and getting ready, they selected teachers from an application pool. There was a project coordinator for the four classrooms and staff members had released time to plan together, reflect, and research. After the initial project was initiated, no new classrooms with the multiage structure were added, even though there was a waiting list each year for families requesting it. The coordinator found that the other teachers in the district wanted nothing to do with the program. They noted the differences between their own and those multiage classrooms. It had become so unique and worlds apart from their own classrooms.

I learned from their experience to stress the similarities rather than the differences so that other professionals might better be able to relate to and understand multiage. We could share the idea that multiage allows us the opportunity to carry out a developmental, child-centered approach to teaching. It supports and carries such an approach one giant step further by giving the gifts of time and continuity.

The following fall we had a multiage "expert" speak to the school community. She presented basic characteristics and reasonings for such a structure; talked about developing a sense of belonging and familiarity; shared examples of children who thrive because of increased self-confidence; discussed time, continuity as an outsider, and friends helping friends; and answered questions. She could concentrate on the objective, informational areas and not get caught up in the personal, emotional aspects involved.

We found at the meeting that many parents who had been part of the multiage classroom the year before were there to answer questions and share first-hand insights. All in all it seemed to educate and disarm many concerns and misgivings about the program.

The spring of that second year I offered a three credit "class" for teachers within my school district who were interested in exploring the multiage concept. Twenty teachers from four elementary schools enrolled. At first I was the expert and shared my knowledge, experiences, and readings. As we moved along, they joined my role of expert very quickly, for as they thought about what they did in their classrooms and why they did it, they discovered their own clarity of philosophy. We discovered many bridges, and unearthed many similarities. While we all had our own way of doing things, we also shared some common themes among us about how children learn and what we were doing about it. They really seemed to understand that multiage gave the structure that complemented the learning and teaching we wanted to support.

This year, my fourth, finds my school with eighty percent of the classrooms multiage. Many parents are vocally supportive. We plan to create a slide show presentation that can be shared with teachers, parents, administrators, and other people who are interested in learning more about our multiage program. It will show what happens in the classrooms as we attempt to explain why we do what we do.

In summary, multiage legitimizes my beliefs and my philosophy. I need to communicate this to others in a way they understand. Doing that keeps presenting new and interesting avenues for me. Research, meetings, slide shows, classes for teachers, writing, and on, and on. I believe in multiage so strongly that I will be going on and on. . . .

" . . . multiage allows us the opportunity to carry out a developmental, child-centered approach to teaching."

Chapter 9

Molly McClaskey

Essex Elementary School
Essex, Vermont

- *classroom community*
- *informality*
- *group meetings*
- *reading*
- *teacher modeling*
- *teacher as learner*
- *conversation*

There is No Front to the Room: Thoughts on Power and Empowerment, and Building a Classroom Community

I started teaching when I was nine years old. My father nailed an old blackboard to the basement wall and I instantly imagined a classroom there. I arranged every old lawn chair and broken table and lined up students: three stuffed bears, a cat with one ear missing, Raggedy Ann, whose clothes were long gone, and all of the others in my misshapen but well-loved collection. Then I taught. I stood at the front with all eyes unblinkingly on me. Mine was the only voice. Such control.

I have never taught like that since. I learned early in my first year of teaching that many educators still think good teaching means quiet rows of busy children, control from the front, and no conversation or movement in the room. I was searching for something more dynamic and interactive. I wanted to create an environment where the students were involved not just with the teacher but with one another.

Developing a Community of Learners

My first two years of teaching were in a small, rural school in Vermont, a low cinder-block structure, plunked squarely in the middle of a cow pasture, just barely fenced off to make room for swings and a basketball hoop. I shared a room with the principal and taught "his" fifth graders in the morning. He taught them in the afternoon when I worked with children of migrant farm families. When I arrived in August to set up the room his large metal desk was at the front, near the blackboard, and twenty-eight wooden desks faced his in perfect rows, filling every inch of the room right to the windows. Being a bold new graduate I couldn't imagine teaching that way and I began moving all the furniture around. I put the student desks in pods of three and four, put the principal's desk to the side, brought in an old rug, two tables from a lawn sale, and covered half the blackboard with fabric to make more display space for student work. It seemed obvious. Now there would be more space for different kinds of activities. It did not occur to me that the principal might feel no need for more classroom space or different kinds of activities. During our first day of inservice he took me aside and said, "You can try teaching with the room set up like this, but as soon as you lose control of the kids we'll put it back my way. I'll tell yah, this group isn't going to be a piece of cake." That first year all twenty-eight fifth graders showed up, several of whom had stayed back, some more than once. Kevin's and Steven's voices were already quite husky. It would be my first multiage experience, although no one intended it that way. Luckily, I never did have to return the desks to straight rows, but we had our share of trying times. The principal observed me very closely through the small window in the door.

The children in this school already knew how to rely on one another. This was a struggling farm community that gathered for town suppers and helped one another get in the hay on summer afternoons. The children were aware of their strengths and weaknesses and were vehemently protective of one another. Joe could already drive a tractor, Katie won the spelling bee every year. There was a well-established social order which was especially obvious at recess time. The children seemed quite comfortable with it, even if there were bullies. Everyone but me knew the ropes. I walked cautiously on their turf, listening, watching, and supporting. I had no choice. They had full control of the social arena at recess time and sometimes during class as well. Some teachers in the building lived in fear of what might get stirred up outside and find its way back into their classrooms.

By November a wrinkle had begun to emerge in our classroom. Things did not work for everyone after all. One new and very capable student, Ann, became the object of the other children's ridicule and a scapegoat for problems. She was not farm toughened and did not operate within the same set of social rules. She was envied by some and disliked by most. She often came in from recess subdued and quiet, no pack of peers with whom to walk in the door. The day she broke into tears at lunch, I intervened and started group discussions about feelings. I explained that we were all entitled to our own feelings and respect from one another. No one should feel hurt without working out the problem. I said that what was occurring now was unfair. No one should feel scared or intimidated.

These first discussions were rocky. Some laughed their way through and others shut down completely, unwilling to speak. Until now our time on the rug had been devoted to sharing our work and talking about plans for the day. After all, the rug itself and sitting side-by-side on it was a revelation for this group. Now, a regular time was set aside for discussions about feelings, and a tight structure for rules was defined. The structure gave some safety to those (almost everyone) new to this realm of communication.

I offered sentences for them to practice and try out. They were used word for word. First we practiced making affirmative statements like, "Ellen, it makes me feel happy when you push me high on the swings," or "Jeff, it makes me feel safe when you stand near me on the jungle gym." When affirmative statements were made comfortably we pushed on and talked about what bothered us. "Joe, when you called me a goody-goody on the bus I felt embarrassed and mad" or, "Sue, when you won't answer me I feel upset and ignored. I don't understand why you won't answer." No one was asked to reply but rather to simply learn how to explain their feelings and receive feedback. Knowing that responses were not expected made the process safer for them. We made lists of synonyms for common feeling words so that words other than bad and good could become a part of their vocabulary. I participated too. It took weeks of practice before we could deal effectively with Ann's feelings.

The Children Take Charge

Control was initially mine. I was the leader modeling how to converse about feelings. When the routine became comfortable, I dropped back and let the discussion take its own shape. I knew the children would not be fully committed unless they owned the meeting, saw it as their own. They gradually took over. They set the time each week and distributed roles, i.e., who would start the meeting, who would check the time, and who would facilitate. I directed subtly from the sidelines by modeling words and sentences they could use, although this was needed less often as the group progressed. I was eventually seen as just another participant. When they assumed responsibility for the meeting (and thus for each other), a dramatic effect was felt in the room.

The honesty and trust that grew allowed people to realize everyone's vulnerability and to recognize the injustice to Ann. When Ann openly discussed her hurt feelings there were many surprised and concerned faces in the group. Some children had experienced similar feelings at one time or another but never spoke up about

"The children were aware of their strengths and weaknesses and were vehemently protective of one another."

100

them. As familiar as the children were with each other, the town was like a big family; their feelings were foreign to one another. Ann came back into the fold with friends and a new sense of trust in her peers. So did everyone else. Tattling virtually disappeared. With regular group meetings there was no need, and the bullies were tamed by their classmates. Problems did not vanish but ignoring them or turning them over to a "tough guy" to solve did. Now everyone had a voice and knew they would have a chance to be heard.

This first year was about community-building, getting the children to talk honestly with one another, and to help each other. It was about control. I was sorting out how to share the control in the classroom without completely stripping myself of it. I was experimenting with routine and the value of limits. I discovered that well-defined structure and expectations enable a teacher to empower children and let go a bit.

I still think about control in the classroom twelve years later. I evaluate myself continually, making adjustments in order to balance teacher and student control, to find enough, but not too much, structure. I go out of my way to share my questions and mistakes with the children and to model imperfection. I want them to accept and respect mistakes as well as achievements. I want them to know I am not in control of all of the information in the room, that I too am a learner. I also want them to discover and utilize one another.

I work at nurturing the expert in every child while also helping children recognize and appreciate the things we do not do well or the things we do differently from one another. When asked a question during work time my response is often, "Who else have you asked?" or "Can you find someone in the room who can help you with that?" The children begin to share the role of assisting and the responsibility of helping one another learn. In multiage classrooms, where students stay with the same teacher for several years in succession, students get quite comfortable assisting one another's learning. The role comes quite naturally, like in one's family. The children are in it together rather than in competition with one another. They gradually learn the difference between telling an answer outright and guiding a peer to his or her own conclusions. They too are engaged in the art of teaching. When the teacher is not the sole authority in the class, children take control of their quest for knowledge.

Balancing Student and Teacher Control

This past year in my multiage class I realized again the relationship between structure and control. While driving home I reflected on the events during writing that day and realized the students had taken control of the assisting roles I once played and modeled earlier in the year. I had hardly noticed the transition. While an emergent

"This first year was about community-building, getting the children to talk honestly with one another, and to help each other."

writer shared his first piece of writing, classmates guided him through the stages of sharing, receiving feedback, and publishing. They had effectively taken control of a writing conference.

He bumped up beside me as I was talking with another child, and nudged my shoulder, giving his usual low grunt. When I looked to my side, Jake, who wore a glazed doughboy look most of the time, was radiant! His blue eyes were bulging and a smile cut across his puffy, dirt-streaked cheeks. "Look it what I made. See it's a book!" He waved several smudged and curled pages in front of my nose. He had been working on these pages for months.

"I see, this is exciting Jake, your first one! Will you read it to me?" (Most would say Jake did not know how to read.) A small crowd had gathered around to hear Jake's story. I called to a few specific people whom I thought might benefit. Ethan, a first grader, was struggling with fine motor control but could conceptualize a complicated story plot. He had a way of frowning on those who couldn't do things. I asked Abby, a second grader, to join us. She was perhaps the brightest in the group. She did everything with ease, yet struggled with peer interactions. I called Nick away from the block area, another first grader, who was on the verge of independent writing and a good buddy to Jake.

Jake had come to our class several months after school started and had trouble settling in and making friends. He spoke very little and communicated aggressively with his overweight body. He had been in five other schools during the previous year and currently lived in an unheated camper behind his grandmother's house with numerous relatives. He often had trouble thinking of things to write about. Hunting with his dad was a recurring theme in his writing and drawing. He had chosen this topic for his first book and had stapled four pages together as he had seen his classmates around him do.

I asked everyone to listen. He read quietly and quickly, " 'Deer Hunten by Jake Conner."

Someone said, "I didn't hear it, Jake, could you read it again?" This time Jake read loudly and with more authority. When he turned the page to go on someone else chimed in, "You forgot to show your cover picture," helping him with the process of sharing. All of this interest in his piece of writing was making Jake shine, he could hardly hold back a smile. He kept rubbing his fingers across his mouth trying to wipe the smile off, like it was in the way, but it crept back each time.

"I went huntin' with my dad. We killed one," he read. He then held the page up to show the illustration and flashed it quickly past everyone. Taylor said, "Slow down Jake, we can't even see your picture." Jake tried again and moved the picture much more slowly. On the next page he read, "The end." And on the last page Jake

"This past year in my multiage class I realized again the relationship between structure and control."

read, "About the Author. Jake Conner is seven years old. He likes to hunt best. He likes his dad."

Everyone applauded, even those who had not joined our impromptu meeting. They had listened from where they were, drawn in by Jake's first sharing ever. I asked, "Does anyone have comments or questions for Jake?"

Abby, our resident writer and artist, raised her hand. She tended to make critical comments about other people's work. For some students this was helpful feedback but not for all. I wondered if she would be able to figure out what information would be most helpful to Jake. Jake called on her. "I like how you made your cover. The colors are really bright," she said. Jake beamed silently, so did I. Kyle was standing right next to Jake and whispered loudly in his ear, "Say thanks, Jake."

Covering his smile with his hand, he looked down and said a muffled, "Thanks."

Nick raised his hand next and Jake recognized it. "I think you're good," Nick commented. Jake thanked him immediately. I asked Nick to clarify himself. We had been practicing giving specific feedback to one another.

"Nick, can you explain what you mean? Do you think he is good at something?"

"Yea, he's gooder than me at being an author."

"He's better than me, too," said Ethan, for whom writing was painstaking, yet he had thought himself well beyond Jake. He hadn't produced a book yet and was in awe now.

"What shows you he's good at being an author, Nick?" I asked.

"It's great how he made that book! And he remembered the 'All About the Author' part too," replied Nick.

Todd, a second grader who was still struggling with fluency in his writing added, "Jake, I used to write about huntin' all the time. I used to write jist like you!" Jake's accomplishment was significant to each person in a slightly different way, and Jake gleaned something new from each comment. He was thrilled to have his work likened to Todd's, an older writer he looked up to. Jake called on a few more hands and then the group went back to the things they had been doing.

I asked Abby to explain to Jake how he could publish his draft. They took off to the writing area where a volunteer mom put Jake's words in print on the computer as he watched. When that was finished Abby explained how to choose a cover and where to put the illustrations.

I joined them to see how things were going and gave Abby a tip about assisting Jake. "Abby, Jake might need to learn about how the illustrations help tell about the story on each page. Can you show

"Staying out of the way is sometimes the biggest challenge for a teacher."

"Now there are many voices, groups of children . . . discussing and cooperating in one another's learning efforts."

him one of your books and explain what I mean?" Abby took off to the shelf of published books and returned with one of hers. Until now Jake's drawings were quick, two colored and not representational. I left but stayed within ear shot to hear how Abby would handle things. We had been working on her tendency to be bossy and do things for people when they already knew how. Her peers disliked her know it all air. Would she take the time to explain this idea or draw the picture for him?

Jake looked through Abby's book with her. He mimicked the feedback he had heard earlier saying," Nice job on that one Abby," and, " I like the colors in this one." Abby showed Jake how her illustrations depicted the words. I had to resist the temptation to jump in and take over. They went back to Jake's book. Jake said, "I'll draw a deer bein' killed here. That's about the story right?" He was rehearsing his thoughts with Abby. She agreed that his idea would describe the words in his story.

When he began the drawing, I could see Abby getting anxious. She could hardly stand it. She wanted to make the drawing her way. She didn't like his rendition. I went back over to them and thanked Abby for her help. "Think I should help him draw the deer?" she asked me as we walked to a different table.

"What do you think, Abby?" I asked.

"Na, he has to learn himself," she replied.

Jake's great learning leap provided insights for others as well as himself. Todd reflected on his own growth as a writer, Ethan was humbled by another's accomplishment, and Abby practiced her assisting skills. A structure for sharing and valuing on another's work was already in place. Peers guided Jake through his first book sharing and one to publishing. I was hardly needed. The children were in control and my job was to provide the foundation so that it could occur and to gently aide those who were assisting Jake without assuming all of the responsibility myself. Staying out of the way is sometimes the biggest challenge for a teacher.

The multiage setting is a natural place to work out a balance between student and adult control. In a mixed-age grouping children are resources for one another and eventually, having been in the room for more than one year, they become experts about how the room works and about the learning process itself. They learn to look to one another for help. Exchange of ideas, working cooperatively, getting fully involved in one's work, and appreciating different learning stages and pace are cultivated and publicly valued in the classroom. These behaviors are the framework upon which the curriculum rests. The classroom becomes a workshop, a studio of artists learning from and supporting one another, and the teacher an integral part, rather than the odd adult out.

Now there is no front, no lone teacher's voice, no unquestioning blank stares. As I outgrew my bears and dolls I also outgrew the need for conventional control and quiet, straight rows. Now there are many voices, groups of children gathered around a project or problem, discussing and cooperating in one another's learning efforts. There is control all right, and a considerable amount of structure. But it is hard to pick it out as such in this context. It does not visibly dominate. Control and structure enable the classroom system to work as it does. Once modeled, reinforced, and practiced, these become a backdrop to the real guts of the classroom, the learning. With routine, structure, and tone well established early in the year, the teacher and students are free to get immersed in the passion of learning.

A Time That Becomes: Anecdotes About Child-Emergent Curriculum and Planning for Spontaneity

Sarah came flying in the door a bit late, hair uncombed, shirt inside-out, her usual state of disarray. She barreled right over to me and asked, in an out of breath voice, "You know what?"

"No, tell me, " I said.

"My grandmother died last night and I got new boots, see?" She lifted one foot so I could have a closer look at the perfectly black, shiny new barn boot.

This is why we have Explore Time first thing each morning. The children come in the door with a whole night of experiences to share. Too often they are asked to forget their out of school lives, and become something different in the classroom. Explore Time is a bridge between home and school. It welcomes children as they are, with whatever is brimming in their thoughts. There is no immediate need to conform to a group discussion or specific task, no demand on them to put away their home world for later. Explore Time is their time, "a time that becomes." It is a time for the teacher to take cues from the children, a time defined by the children.

The teacher composes a structure and children improvise on it. Learning areas such as: sand, water, art, books and tapes, drama, writing, science, etc., are available as well as a few spin-offs from the previous day's work or the topic currently being studied by the whole group. A child might choose none of these and start something altogether different or simply spend time chatting with a friend. It is a time children orchestrate and direct. It is an opportunity for the teacher to stand back and practice taking off the director's hat so that children may wear it.

Rick and Evan were great planners and inventors. They often came in the door knowing what they wanted to do and got right to it. They arrived one morning toting a huge bag of equipment. In it were various screw drivers, pulleys, rubber bands, nuts and bolts, batteries, and pliers. Then the beginnings of a small automated cart-contraption emerged. Their morning project would be a continuation of work they had begun at Evan's house after school the day before. Soon two other pals joined them and began to contribute ideas. When I came over to look they explained that they wanted their vehicle to plow and also move small rocks. I left for a while and came back several times throughout Explore Time to observe their trials, to ask questions, and hear how they were thinking about

106

the project. We had been experimenting with tracks, balls and inclines for several days and I noted that concepts like momentum and its relationship to weight were being investigated as they worked. After several mornings of serious work they announced loudly to everyone that their invention was ready for a test run. We all gathered at the rock pile on the side of the playground to watch the little machine crawl slowly to a small stone, scoop it up, and deposit it again. Cheers resounded. Rick and Evan wore expressions like they had just landed a rocket on Jupiter!

Blending Structure and Flexibility

Explore Time offers teacher and student the chance to ease in, find a niche and get absorbed. It is a time when children review, revise, and reflect further on work from the previous day. An informal structure is provided for students. The teacher works in tandem with the learner, paying close attention to the child's self-initiated pursuits; guiding while trusting the learner's impulses; and setting routine while leaving room for spontaneity and direction from the children.

Through a graceful blending of structure and flexibility the curriculum emerges from the children. Explore Time helps the teacher develop a whole picture of a child as well as notice the potential hooks for the child's learning. Hooks are those interests expressed by the child, things that excite the learner and could lead to in-depth work on a topic. Whole class projects are conceived during Explore Time. The teacher gets involved in conversations with children, listens in, and watches in order to observe a child's interests and tendencies., and uses the information for planning. Explore Time provides the teacher with raw data and a resource file full of possible themes to pursue throughout the year.

Explore Time can last anywhere from a half-hour to two hours. Some days a strong direction is set by the children and rather than interrupt, we continue. On any given day, Explore Time might become the entire morning's work. On other days it is just an entry point, a way to settle in and gently move from home to school. I extend Explore Time when the majority of the group is involved in something we can sink into for a while. It happens when the work at hand is derived from an activity of the previous day, or when a child's serendipitous discovery is enough to carry us through the morning. When something seems worthy of everyone's attention and will provide ample interesting content and further exploration, we run with it. One morning an idea for a new class research topic was hatched when a child arrived late carrying something from home. Explore Time was redirected by this surprise and by the children's immediate fascination. The study steered our mornings for several weeks. In this way the curriculum emerged from a child's treasure from home.

"Explore Time offers teacher and student the chance to ease in, find a niche and get absorbed."

Following the Children's Lead

"Ms. McClaskey, look over there," came Taylor's excited shout. I looked in the direction of everyone's stare and saw a hauntingly beautiful silver-gray skull peering in the doorway from the hall. Several students passing our door had also stopped to notice. It was Ian arriving late to school. Everyone was so charged with excitement that Explore Time activities were dropped and we gathered around Ian to hear all about it.

Ian explained how he had soaked the skull in Clorox early that morning to get the smell out so that his mom would let him bring it to school. Then it smelled so strongly from the Clorox that he couldn't wear it right away. "My mom let me come late so it could dry out in the sun. Now it doesn't smell too bad," he reported. He lifted the perfectly intact skull from the top of his head and demonstrated how the jaw was hinged. He pointed out the enormous teeth. Others wanted to perch the skull on their heads and Ian helped get it on and off several heads. We touched its smooth weather worn crevices and speculated about the purpose of each nook and bump. As the awe and amazement began to ebb, I puzzled in my teacher mind about how to proceed with the morning. Going back to Explore Time activities would seem dull after this. As I contemplated an activity we might do with the skull, Nick challenged Ian. "I have an even bigger one at home. My dad found it near the manure pile," he said. Ian suggested we weigh and measure his and then do the same with Nick's, if he brought it to class. Our morning's work was set before us. Explore Time became a morning of math experiences, thanks to Ian's idea.

Armed with the cow skull and some past experience with weight and measurement, we decided on a plan. We estimated first and recorded our guesses. Then Rick went down the hall to borrow the scales from the nurse. We weighed the skull and calculated diameter and length with string. Many trials later we agreed on measurements and compared them to our estimates. When this was completed the room was buzzing with conversation about bones and skulls others had at home. Ian's skull launched a larger research study for the whole class.

As I drove home that afternoon my mind was racing with plans. I knew bones would be a terrific topic for a class study.

> 1. There was plenty of interest. Nearly everyone had found a bone or skull somewhere in their travels, and those they had kept would come to school tomorrow.
> 2. It would be easy to extend the topic and tie it in to related sub-themes, like a study of the human skeleton, body systems, bones and skeletons in literature, or archeology.
> 3. I knew there was enough substance to the topic so that children could research some part fully.

4. I knew the topic was broad enough to challenge children on many different levels.

5. I knew our library had some materials and that I could find others.

6. I knew math, science, and language arts could be easily interwoven.

7. The timing was perfect. We were not in the midst of another theme at the moment.

8. I knew I was intrigued with the idea, but more importantly,

9. This was not a contrived or forced topic. It would work because bones were familiar yet also mysterious, full of unknowns.

My planning is often guided by an event like this from the day. I make plans tentatively, thinking about what we could do once a topic has emerged. Tentative planning might seem like an incongruous combination, but it assures that there will be room for input from the children. It requires flexibility and the ability to change course mid-stream. It demands that the teacher listen, encourage, and give attention to the children's interests and expressed ideas. It means taking clues from the children to find out what is intriguing to them. It means designing an overview and realizing things may not go the way you have planned. It means day-to-day planning based on each day's work with the children. Tentative planning means sharing the responsibility of guiding where the topic will go with the children.

When I got home I made a web (some call this a brainstorm) about bones, as I would do with the children the following morning. This gives me ideas for where our study might wander and how we might integrate other subject matter. I thought through several activities we could do and planned a sequencing and comparing activity for the bones that would arrive the following morning. I knew I would plan more extensively later, but wanted to keep the momentum going. I planned for tomorrow's bones and spent the rest of my evenings at home that week researching the topic. I reviewed plans from previous weeks to see what skills we were working on that might be integrated. I reviewed resources from the library, and read and learned about bones myself. I chose books to read aloud to the class and some to leave in the room for resources. I chose books some children might read themselves for independent research. I brainstormed possible individual research topics and things we might build or create together. I made a list of resources I wanted to find to bring into the class, like a full-sized human skeleton, x-rays, etc. I pored over song and poetry books to find related text we could use for language lessons. List after list took shape. These lists and webs are my plans. When the planning is complete I feel prepared for the unexpected, the things I haven't thought of

"Hooks are those interests expressed by the child, things that excite the learner and could lead to in-depth work on a topic."

which will undoubtedly occur. Plans made, I feel comfortable putting them aside should something more immediate and important arise from the children.

Next day nearly everyone arrived with bones, of every size and shape, from pork chop to skunk. For the few who hadn't found any, there were those who brought bags full to share. The task was to examine the bones closely and compare them. Everyone, ages six to eight, lay their bones on the rug. Then we talked about what we saw. I wrote the describing words they were using on chart paper as they discussed the collection. We would get back to these adjectives at some later point. They would make a meaningful lesson on describing words during a future writing period. We sorted the bones in a variety of ways, then ordered them by size. This brought on debate over which bones were biggest, the longest ones or those largest all over. Next I asked each person to carefully draw one of the bones and measure it. "Draw everything you notice about your bone," I said. Clipboards, pencils, drawing paper, bones, and magnifiers in hand, each found a place to work. As they broke off from the larger group I watched them finding the right work space. Michelle and Nicole were under the easel, Lizzy, Abby and Casey were at one table, Ethan and Taylor were at another, and Nick and Ian were in the block area on the floor. They naturally found people with whom they could work. (Earlier in the year this would not have happened so smoothly and required input from the teacher and practice.) Ethan helped Taylor, a younger student, see that the string for measuring had to be held at the end of the bone in order to get an accurate measure. Lauren was not clear which way to measure, around or down the length. She and Michelle, the older of the two, discussed what we had all done yesterday with Ian's skull and decided to take both measurements. Nick asked Ian to help him cut his string; the scissors wouldn't work. Then Ian noticed Nick's string was much shorter than his and yet they had measured the same bone. "Nick, how'd you get this so short?" Ian asked.

"I'll show you," Nick lay the string on the cow skull between the two eye sockets.

"Oh, I see," said Ian, "Mine is the whole length, yours is from eye to eye, neat."

"Yea," said Nick. When it came time to display and label their measurements, Ian helped Nick by taking dictation for his labels.

The children assisted one another during the course of the activity. Those who had been in the class the previous year were well acquainted with how to get help as well as offer it, and they modeled this for the younger group. It's hard to imagine teaching without this kind of team work! How could I possibly help everyone at once?

Everything from human to turtle skeletons was pieced together. It's amazing what help the local high school science department can be. They provided us with boxes of human bones which we eventually pieced together to make a complete human skeleton. We learned about archeology and bone preservation, and investigated differences in shapes, sizes, and purposes. We investigated joints, sockets, and specific bones. A bone specialist visited the class and brought diagrams and models. We were off and running!

Commitment to a topic is more profound when students make decisions and guide learning along with the teacher. Ian felt empowered by his skull and his classmates' interest in it. He directed our first morning's work, and, with his contagious enthusiasm, a new class project began.

Learning and empowerment are interdependent. Together they make the learning process significant and meaningful. The more we learn, the more empowered and in control we are. Conversely, the more empowered we are, the more passionate and engaged in learning we can become. Isn't this what teaching and learning are all about?

"Learning and empowerment are interdependent. Together they make the learning process significant and meaningful."

"You Did It All Morning?": A Discussion of Time and Timing in the Classroom

We were involved in an investigation of water in the dead of winter one year. The theme was inspired by an icicle dripping from the school roof outside our window. We were a few weeks into the topic when the teacher across the hall stuck her head in the door during her lunch break. She said, with eyebrows raised and admonishing tone, "Are they still making that same water cycle diagram? You did it all morning didn't you?"

"Yes," I replied. "Want to see the underground stream they added?" She did not come in.

From the doorway she just shook her head and said, "I don't know how you find the time with all we have to teach." Then she was gone.

There is time. All the stuff we had to teach was embedded in our study of the water cycle. It was just harder to recognize. I wish I had shown her my clipboard of records showing the skills children were practicing through a variety of water-related experiments and activities. I wish I had shown her my plans. One web shows the many subjects integrated into the topic, and another shows the variety of activities we might do and what skills are practiced in each. Another lists the literature we will use.

I wish I had told her not to expect a change of scenery the next time she popped her head in the door, because we would probably study water for a month or more. We were creating a living diagram on the bulletin board near the water table as we explored concepts of the water cycle. This project alone would take two weeks. I should have told her that a class discussion had evolved that morning after someone noticed the water in their margarine dish had evaporated. I did not explain that the morning was taken up with a deeper look at evaporation than the previous day, or that new experiments had been set up since yesterday. She did not know that children wrote about their discoveries for forty minutes earlier that day. We were keeping science journals, called water logs. Activities, results, questions, and ideas were recorded regularly in them. Sometimes we wrote at the end of a work time or at the end of the day to summarize what we had done. Sometimes I planned a specific graphing or record-keeping activity to be logged in the journal. This particular morning I asked the group to brainstorm all we had learned so far about water. The children generated a lengthy list. Then I asked them to choose one or two items from the list and write about their understanding of the concept, experiment, or word they had chosen. I was assessing what they had gleaned to this point in our study and how much detail they were able to recall and generalize.

"Time and Enough of It"

The teacher across the hall did not stay long enough to see children learning about cloud formation with steam and ice, an experiment that we had until now only read about. Today was different from yesterday while also the same. But how could my colleague notice the changes without spending time in the room? A different group had circulated to the water cycle diagram and were now asking about how water is emitted from leaves into the air. They embarked on an experiment to find out if transpiration occurs in pine needles as it does in flat leaves. One group was investigating how water droplets travel on different surfaces and another was hypothesizing and testing floating and sinking properties of different objects. Elsa had finished a research piece on lightning and was drawing the three kinds of lightning she had investigated. A small group had resumed work with clay boats in a tub of water. These explorations take time and flow from one day into the next. Elsa was much more involved in her lightning project than she had expected to be, partly because she had ample time to think about it and share her findings with peers. Answers and new questions are not conveniently derived in forty minute periods. When children are fully involved in an activity they want to keep going, they do not want the period to end. There must be time for the unexpected.

Time and enough of it is essential if discovery and child-initiated learning are to be part of the learning process. Worktime must be long enough that children can get lost in what they are doing. Depth, meaning, and absorption are not realized in forty minute intervals.

When a child stays with a task or topic for several days or weeks, a different kind of learning occurs. A child needs repeated experiences with materials and concepts in order to get beyond newness, beyond the messing about stage. It is through repeated experiences over time that hypothesizing, experimentation, trial and error, discovery, application, and extension become part of the learning process. It is the duration of a topic that ignites real learning and involvement.

So we *do* take whole mornings or afternoons on a single topic and many weeks on the same theme. Parents and colleagues do not always recognize the other disciplines (math, language arts, problem solving, etc.) and skills that are a part of the project. Careful records must be kept in order to show parents, administrators, or colleagues why the topic can consume the whole morning for several weeks. If math is not a significant part of what we are doing one day, I devote

"Time and enough of it is essential if discovery and child-initiated learning are to be part of the learning process."

> *"In this way our classroom activities resemble learning in the real world."*

a large chunk of the next day to math. Generally our worktime has an emphasis, perhaps math/science for several days, then language arts/social studies. Other subject areas like drama or cooking are interwoven when and where they fit. Not all days or parts of days are left wide open for such chunking of time. I have to work around specials, but whenever possible, every few days, I leave wide blocks of time for theme work. When possible, I intentionally avoid breaking up the day by subject.

Learning that Runs Deep

In this way our classroom activities resemble learning in the real world. When going to buy milk for my home I do not classify the trip to the grocery store as a reading, math, or social studies experience. These disciplines naturally overlap in the world and inform one another. We want children to see the relationship between school learning and real-life experiences and to see the purpose in their school activities. Experiences in the classroom are purposefully interconnected and involve children in real-life ideas and problems.

Time is a prerequisite for meaningful, extended theme work with children. Teachers and children need more than single class periods in which to work. Schools traditionally schedule teaching/ learning time in thirty or forty minute units. This has shaped how teachers teach and how children learn for years. Regardless of what they are in the midst of, children have come to expect a subject to bluntly end after forty minutes. Arbitrary ending of class periods inhibits commitment to a task and prevents a child from getting deeply involved in the work at hand. Children have learned to hurry through work in order to complete tasks before the end of a period. When something is finished it is often forgotten, there is not time to get back to it. I am afraid children are learning that there is no time for real depth and that shallow activities, unrelated to what has occurred before or after, are what learning is all about—short and finished—like a TV episode.

I look for ways to slow down and draw out the learning process. I look for reasons to ask children to take a second or third look at their work. I want them to re-examine and remember what they are doing from one day to the next. I want them to get beyond the surface and get absorbed. I intentionally plan for continuity and duration.

Mural Making: The Interdependence of Process and Product

We had embarked on an investigation of animals we had seen in Vermont habitats. The students were well into their research projects when we started a mural depicting the animals and their homes. I put out several boxes of different sized paper scraps, fabric, felt, tissue paper, metallic paper, wallpaper, and the like. First we met as a group to discuss a general plan for the mural. I asked things like, "What do you want it to look like?" and "What should we include?" I made rough sketches of their ideas on chart paper as the discussion evolved. I encouraged each child to figure out what he would make and where it might be located in the mural. Every child knew where to start.

There is a difference between mindless copying from books and using books effectively for learning. I had encouraged the children to go back to the resource books they had been using in order to find illustrations and photos as models for their work. The goal was for children to observe as much detail about the animal of study and then make their animal as life-like as possible. I was looking for creations that would describe how the animal truly looks and lives; drawings and cutouts that would indicate what the children had noticed and learned about their animal.

Then the making began. I asked the children to first sketch, using the resource books in order to help them observe closely and slow their pace, a rehearsal of their work. Sketching, like a first draft, encourages revision and conversation. It helps children realize the time and attention required in quality work. We made great progress that day, and I knew then the mural making would last several full mornings.

Next morning, the majority of children pulled out their unfinished animals right away when they arrived. Explore Time was very focused as it often is when a topic is under way. Large trees were being painted for the forest habitat and an intricate paper beaver lodge with entrance and exit tunnels was being glued to the blue paper pond. Those who finished one item went to the mural where they discussed with peers where it should go. I helped people determine what to do next, found appropriate materials, and asked questions when it seemed necessary. "Do you think the owl's feet hold on in this direction or the other way? Let's look it up." I helped find resource books and sometimes pointed out the things I was also learning. "Look at how big a fox den is. I hadn't realized

• different kinds of learning
• art as a medium of expressing
• continuity
• holistic perspective
• deep learning
• active learning
• Explore Time

115

that before." Sometimes I stopped everything and asked the group to step back and have a look at the mural. "What does it need?" I might ask. We would quickly brainstorm an additional list. Once when we had stopped to assess our work in progress it was noticed that there was no sun. Good heavens!

After our usual half-hour Explore Time it was clear that everyone was engaged and so we continued. We worked on the mural for the next three mornings. I knew there was plenty of meaningful work to sustain us so I abandoned my plans to do a teacher-directed activity on endangered species in Vermont. I knew it would keep. I am glad I did because I had a chance to hear about how, just last night, Ethan had called a neighbor who hunts wild turkeys. Ethan was researching wild turkeys. He had asked the man about the animal and did he have any left over body parts he could loan him to take to school. Ethan remembered the phone call with Mr. Mosier some time in the middle of the morning and suddenly exclaimed, "Oh yea, Ms. McClaskey, want to see the turkey parts I got from Mr. Mosier next door?" We gathered about Ethan's backpack to view each piece as it was drawn from the bag, first the foot, then a skull, and lastly, a wing. After some discussion, Ethan made labels for each part and displayed them on the science shelf with a sign that read, "ETHAN'S TURKEY BODY PARTS MUSEUM, PLEASE HANDLE CAREFULLY."

Explore Time is most often extended when excitement and interest carries over from one day to the next. A whole group investigation builds momentum and the children naturally gravitate to their unfinished work from the previous day. Sometimes this kind of continuity and perserverance directs Explore Time, or the whole morning, for days on end.

After four days of concentrated effort, the mural was nearly complete. The final phase was labeling the animals and their homes. We label our murals and drawings occasionally during the year to sharpen the children's attention to detail. While labeling their work, children sometimes discover something they want to revise. Upon re-examining his bobcat while making a label, Rick thought the neck too long. He reshaped it and then completed his label. Mia realized she had made a different kind of mouse than the one she had made a label for, and went back to the resource book to see the actual color of a field mouse. Labeling is a way of going back to one's work with a critical eye. It heightens the child's sense of audience and desire for others to understand what has been made. It is also a valuable assessment tool for the teacher. I could observe those children who chose to revise and why, and I watched the way in which children used their resource materials. I could see whether or not children had made the connection between the animals, their homes, and their habitats.

"Explore Time is most often extended when excitement and interest carries over from one day to the next."

A Blend of Process and Product

Murals are a rich blend of process and product. Without emphasizing the importance of the product, everyone is keenly aware of the purpose of the mural and its high visibility in the classroom. Children know it is a showpiece. Yet, while in process, there is vibrant discussion, comparison, planning, revision, decision making, creating, and experimenting taking place. Concern about what it will be in the end does not diminish the children's minute-to-minute or day-to-day involvement in the process. In fact, a certain amount of attention to product vitalizes their absorption and effort. When the product is highly valued by the children, there is a stronger commitment to the task and the children's work is more detailed and in-depth. The product becomes a masterpiece and children feel they have been artists when it is complete. Mural making strikes a complementary balance between product and process.

On day five we all agreed the mural was finished. During quiet reading Michelle came up quietly and whispered, "I think it's neat, don't you?" as she gazed at the multi-layered wall of animals in and about their homes.

"What do you really like about it Michelle?" I asked.

"The bobcat coming out of the rotten log and the field mice in their burrow. It almost looks like a real bobcat, don't you think?"

I agreed. "I like how he showed the rotting log with fungus on it, like it was at the Audubon Center, do you remember the fungus we saw?" I asked. Michelle nodded in agreement.

There was an overwhelming sense of accomplishment in the room. Parents were later invited to view group plays, written research projects, and the mural. The room was spilling over with our Vermont Animals Project and the children were spilling over with pride as they took their parents on a tour of their work.

"When the product is highly valued by the children, there is a stronger commitment to the task and the children's work is more detailed and in-depth."

"What Did You Do in School Today Dear?":

Talk Among Children, Parents, and Teachers

"What did you do in school today dear?" must be one of the most frequent questions asked of children when they step in the door after school.

"Nothin'," is probably the most common reply.

Parents often rely on their children's account of the school day to learn about school programs. Report cards four times per year and parent-teacher conferences once or twice offer only one kind of information about school. Parents miss out on information which would help them talk about school with their children, and teachers shortchange themselves when their programs go unexplained. Daily papers going home from the classroom do little to educate parents. I used to find papers and projects trampled in the corner of the bus or at the bottom of a child's cubby; worse yet, in our trash can, never even having left the classroom. I sometimes asked the group if anyone had shown their work to a parent that night.

I cringed to hear what became of their work after all of the hours, days, or sometimes weeks we had worked. Papers and projects were left at the sitter's, or at the bottom of a backpack, or someone at home had thrown them away not realizing their importance. These are pieces of the child's day and demonstrate a child's learning and growth. They show practice and application of skills in math or language arts, or a combination of subjects. But how are parents to know the significance of these projects without some kind of guidance? It's no wonder they get the wrong idea or have no idea at all about what goes on at school. Who explained the value of a theme on bones to the parents? Who described the skills children learned while weighing and measuring them? How could they have known the strings in their child's backpack were from a measuring activity? How would a parent know what to interpret from multiple sketches of bones? Maybe it looks like an art lesson, or even a waste of time.

Communicating with Parents

Teachers undermine themselves by keeping information to themselves. Hours of preparation cannot possibly be appreciated or noticed if the results are misunderstood or overlooked. We are obligated to explain or live with what gets discussed at the supermarket by an uninformed public. Myths are created that way! "Noise" and activity level can stand out first to a parent rather than the learning taking place.

Notions of children moving around the room and an atmosphere thriving on conversation and student choice are new and frightening ideas to some parents. It is flat out wrong in the minds of some. There is need to educate parents as well as administrators and colleagues about why and what we do. Teaching several ages together, a multiage program, is new to some schools and parents. These programs require an even greater emphasis on communication and education in the community in order to debunk misconceptions. Parents expect schools to be familiar, to resemble their memories of schooling. When they see or hear about different methods and their children do not bring home typical daily papers, it is difficult for them to trust that learning is taking place.

Communication with parents can start with the children and their attitude about their work. I begin by training the children to value their own work. The children learn to discuss one another's pieces, revise them, and celebrate the final copy or project with worthy exhibition and praise. Before work goes home we talk about what was learned in the theme or project. Sometimes I make a list as they discuss all we did and learned. We talk about what they want to do with their finished pieces once they arrive home. Some fear they will have no place at home to show their work and choose to display their work in the school library or office. Most children think about a place to hang it at home and go home with a plan. We also discuss how to share their work with someone at home. I ask the children what they want to tell their parent(s) or sibling about their work. For some, who will have no audience at home, I invite an adult within the school to be surrogate parent, and the child has a private sharing at school. The children have, in this way, become better conduits of information about their learning and convey pride, knowledge, and a sense of importance about their work.

Meaningful communication with home requires more than this. A direct link is needed between teacher and parent. I also write project letters that are usually attached directly to the child's work. In the letter I explain the project or work arriving home. I outline what was learned, and what processes were used to get there. Sometimes I label the children's work so that parents will know what subject areas were explored through the project, i.e., math, language arts, etc. At the conclusion of a long study, work is collected and sent home as a package or scrapbook, with an explanation so that parents can see how the investigation unfolded from beginning to end and observe a progression of their child's work. I tell about the skills and subject matter covered. Sometimes I include the charts, word lists, and brainstorms generated by the children during the topic. I leave room in these letters to thank parents who volunteered or sent materials to class. I provide parents with ample information so they can engage their children in conversation about school at home.

Newsletters are another way to reach parents. These are less formal than a project letter. They briefly describe what we are currently studying. I ask for volunteers and resources related to our topic, and invite suggestions and participation from home. When a theme is just beginning, I look for ways children can share information with their parents. Some of our best activities have come from ideas generated at home. To encourage this kind of involvement I might include in the newsletter a questionnaire or series of questions about the topic that we have brainstormed together. I include quotations from children or brief snip-its from articles of interest. Children do artwork wherever it fits.

Dispelling the Myths

Sometimes, despite all of this extra public relations work, people formulate opinions about classrooms based on incorrect information or hearsay, and often do not ask or visit in order to get an accurate picture. I find most questions about the multiage program arise from parents with children in other classes, unrelated in any way to my room. They have heard or noticed something and did not understand it. These parents, though not directly related to my classroom, need information too. When any program, multiage or other, is misunderstood it affects the whole school climate. A school-wide newsletter can help by keeping the school community informed of programs throughout the building. It is important that parents feel they are involved in a cohesive, supportive, school environment. In some schools, teachers contribute brief sections to the school newsletter each week or month. I also take any opportunity to explain things to questioning parents, whether or not their children are in my classroom. One evening at a parent informational meeting, I learned firsthand that parents were misinformed about the multiage program. It was 9 p.m. after a regular school day, and I could have avoided the conversation, but I felt compelled to respond.

I saw her approaching from the other side of the room, her eyes riveted on me. Some of the teachers had just given a presentation on the first grade curriculum to the P.T.O. Parents were milling about drinking coffee and eating brownies. A school board member came over to within a few inches of my face, so I could smell her lipstick, and said, "This answered some questions for people but still no one asked about discipline, and that's what everybody who calls me wants to know about."

"I wish they had asked. It's a good thing to talk about," I replied, "What do you think people want to know?"

> *"There is need to educate parents as well as administrators and colleagues about why and what we do."*

120

"Well," she said, "A lot of 'em say when they go by your 1-2, (multiage) doorway there's always much more noise coming from that room and no discipline. The kids are all over the place. I've noticed it myself some days." I was happy to have the opportunity to explain to her the importance of conversation, movement, and choice making. I wanted to say, "You're right, there is more noise." But be careful, leave as little room for misinterpretation as possible. I explained that I thought children should experience both quiet and busy times, and understand the boundaries of both. I told her there is control or discipline in either situation and that the limits have been established by the teacher. I praised her for taking the time to ask in order to get the correct story. I also knew she would share this conversation with a good many others on the telephone. I was laying important groundwork.

I explained that for the person passing by, it is hard to know what the content and context of the noise is, and that's what really counts. "Is it really noise?" I asked her, "or are the children planning or experimenting with something? Is it children jabbering about someone's sleep-over party at an inappropriate time, or is it small groups excitedly discussing their next dramatic presentation from the myths we have been studying? Is it a conferencing time when small groups confer about writing or books they are reading? This can be a noisy and highly productive time. Or is it children enthusiastically trying an experiment and shouting with excitement when it works? It is important to visit and see what the activity is." I explained that I have different expectations for the noise level and movement at different times during the day. Reading time, for example, is quiet and children move about less often. A livelier worktime has more movement and normal voices. I said that conversation is a learning tool as are pencil and paper and must be used and practiced like anything else. I encourage kid talk and teach children how to use conversation for learning. It is an important skill throughout life.

Building Good Communication Skills

Conversation is one way children in a multiage classroom benefit from the diverse developmental levels in the room. Hearing one another's ideas and opinions opens the door to new possibilities for those listening in or not quite ready, but intrigued with the concepts being discussed. Good communication skills are vital to learning and living. I encourage children to clarify their thinking through conversation so that everyone can understand them. The children learn to ask one another specific questions and to expand on the ideas of others. Sharing ideas is basic to a healthy learning environment and world. Through talk, children learn to value one another as resources.

"Conversation is one way children in a multiage classroom benefit from the diverse developmental levels in the room."

I encourage conversation and plan activities which will foster group problem solving or planning, whether it be comparing bones from one another's pastures or talking about where to show transpiration in the water cycle diagram. Children experiment with and rehearse social skills, share and revise thoughts, and plan and play through conversation. It offers a window through which the teacher can view a child's thinking process and feelings. It must be practiced and perfected.

Yes, there is noise at certain times of the day, but let's call it talk, because it is often meaningful and quite intentional.

Just Leave Me Alone

Kevin jumped up from his chair, his face as round and red as a balloon, broke his pencil in half and crumpled his paper into a tight mass. He burst into tears." "I hate this," he screeched. I dashed over in time to catch him before he knocked into someone's block structure. He was shaking and sobbing uncontrollably. I put my hands on his shoulders and walked him to the reading area.

"Kevin, sit for a while. I'll come talk with you when the others go to lunch. Don't worry about your paper." He sat down on the rug, head buried in his hands. Gradually his whole body caved in making a tight little lump.

When the room was empty I approached and sat facing him on the floor. He would have shrunk from a hug or any closeness now. He needed his own space and did not want his frustration glossed over for a hug. "You must be feeling angry right now," I said, acknowledging his mood.

A muffled, "Yea," came from his balled up body.

I opened and flattened the crumpled final copy and left it on the floor. "What should we do?"

"Just leave me alone," came the sniffled reply.

"I want to be with you right now and tell you something. It's okay to be upset sometimes. I feel angry too at times. I don't mind that you're angry."

"So?"

"I love you, Kevin," I said.

Wet eyes peeked out from his sweaty cave. Tears streamed down his stained face. "You do?" he asked incredulously. Then relief. His shoulders and back straightened, he rubbed his eyes and face, hiding a soggy, slight, smile.

I wanted to respect his emotions and let him keep them, yet diffuse the storm so that we could talk. I am not one for cute, adoring phrases, but I knew I had to confront Kevin with love. Love was scattered and hurtful in his home right now, and he did not know who cared for him anymore.

Kevin and I had faced off about completing tasks numerous times before. His avoidance of completion had been a common power struggle between us. I knew we had to get back to the business of the final draft. But tomorrow morning would be soon enough. Today, we had accomplished a lot.

The next morning he came in the room tentatively, checking me out. He normally came in like a dirt bike without a muffler. Today he was quiet, just watching. Would I still care, had I forgotten what

123

I had said yesterday? He was too afraid to ask. Undoubtedly he would test to see where we stood if I did not let him know. I came over and put my hands on his shoulder. Looking at him straight on I asked, "How's it going?"

"Okay," he said hesitantly, with eyes on his feet.

I kneeled down and looked right in his eyes. "Are we still buddies?"

"Yup!" he said with a smile. Now he knew I remembered. He settled down to complete the final draft. More importantly he warmed to me. We had never had the kind of easy going conversations about any old thing that I did with most others in the room. He used to seek me out to give a correct answer but not to chat. When we did talk, he was uneasy and in a rush to get back to what he was doing. Now he saddled up close several times each day to tell me something or just to be there, close by. He felt unconditionally cared for. Now I could put my arm around him and he would not shrug it off.

Developing Friendship Making Skills

Kevin was not suddenly transformed. He had outbursts, but less frequently. He struggled with friend making and did not know how to get involved with a group of peers. He was awkward and resorted to ruining people's creations or annoying small groups as a means of getting attention. He blurted out his opinions and answers before anyone in the group had a chance to speak. He needed to prove himself, even if it meant losing potential friends. Some days I wanted to tape his mouth or I wished he would be absent. He never missed a day.

He often smelled like he had forgotten to use the bathroom, even though he was seven. This did not help in the friend making arena. His mother and father had recently broken up and Kevin seemed more fragmented than ever. We would be together for the next two years because this was a multiage classroom, and I knew I had time to delve into Kevin's social and emotional needs without compromising his academic growth. I also knew this could be a long two years together unless we came to terms.

Once Kevin felt safe with me we could work on his other relationships. He knew I would be there no matter what his behavior, but he did not have this same confidence in peers. His behavior brought on rejection and negative feedback. He did not know the warm feeling of having and trusting a friend. He had only a vague notion of friendship and what he was working toward.

Friendship making skills became our emphasis for the rest of the year. For months I listened to how he spoke to others, how he entered conversations, how he reacted when a peer criticized or corrected him. I was still recording his progress in reading, math and other subjects, but social skills were the priority. I knew we

> "Now he saddled up close several times each day to tell me something or just to be there, close by."

could focus attention on social skills now and pick up additional curriculum skills, if needed, in the time ahead. I knew that feeling comfortable with himself and with peers would have a larger impact on his success as an adolescent and adult than being able to tell temperature or understand the water cycle.

A multiage setting affords children and teachers time. It allows the teacher time to work within the child's natural pace of development. When children are with a teacher for more than one year the teacher need not hurry the child through academic or social stages, nor does the teacher have to fit everything in before June.

Patterns in a child's development are more easily observed when teachers have a span of several years to work with the same group of children. The natural and subtle unevenness of a child's growth can be more apparent to a teacher working in a multiage program. There is time to recognize when a child's social needs are more important than academic, and time to seriously devote to them.

Kevin practiced friendship making skills intensely and had the benefit of a second year with the same teacher. He would operate within the same set of guidelines and did not have to renegotiate rules and love with a new teacher the following year. A change in peer group and teacher would have been devastating for Kevin and would have undermined a whole year of work. He benefited from the continuity of peers, classroom structure, and teacher expectations.

Many children deal with multiple child care arrangements and experience a fragmented day outside of school. The multiage classroom provides bonding, a sense of family, and a feeling of rootedness which can be counted on from one year to the next. The extra measure of familiarity and predictability gives children comfort and added confidence for learning and risk taking. This was clearly the case for Kevin. Our classroom was a safety net for him at a time when his family was coming unglued. It was a place where he could risk the difficult work of making friends with peers who knew him well and would be there for him again another year.

I listened relentlessly to his attempts with friends and intervened often. I stopped conversations mid-stream and offered ideas or sentence frames for Kevin to borrow. Kevin had just approached the block area (his favorite place) and started grabbing Evan's tow truck. I hurried over and said, 'Evan, Kevin needs to practice how to ask for that truck. Kevin, you could try, "Evan, when you're finished with the tow truck can I use it?' or, 'Evan, will you be finished with the tow truck soon?'" Sometimes the children offered suggestions for Kevin. I insisted he mimic the words each time. Gradually he realized his errors, especially when he saw me approaching, and attempted to correct himself without my help. Slowly, very slowly, the words became his own.

"Friendship-making skills became our emphasis for the rest of the year."

125

Becoming Part of a Group

One day Kevin was watching three boys experimenting with our water clock, trying to change how much time it could keep. (We were involved in a study of time.) Normally he would have blasted into the group, shown his idea (usually a great one), and left, with the group members angry that their ideas were disregarded and that he had messed things up. He didn't seem to know a graceful way of getting in. This time, however, he sat watching on the side, dying to take part but holding back. I came over quietly and whispered, "Ask them to tell you what they're doing."

Kevin approached, scratching his head nervously. "Watcha doing?" he asked. The three boys explained that they thought it took too long for the water to drip through the bucket into the jar below. They wanted to be able to calculate more time with the clock we had made during the school day. They were right, our experiment had not worked the way I had envisioned it. I was glad they wanted to tackle the problem. Kevin suddenly pushed passed Leo, who was explaining, and grabbed the dripping water bucket. The strings holding it from the ceiling snapped and water sloshed everywhere.

"KEVIN!" they all shouted at once.

"Now it's wrecked," Michael said. Kevin was ready to drop everything and run, but I was right behind him now. Many others in the class had gathered to see what the commotion was all about.

"Let's help Kevin figure out what he could have done differently." By this time the class knew I was helping, or training, Kevin to enter into projects and friendships appropriately. They were willing to help too.

"He shoulda waited to see what we were trying. We were here first!" said Michael. "It's a mess. It's all wrecked."

"He shouldn't have grabbed. It was too rough. It all broke. He'll get a turn. He has to wait though," insisted Leo. "Now he has to clean up." Kevin's actions were often abrupt and uncontrolled. Sometimes the accidents were unintentional, but he did not know what to do once they occurred.

I did not have to say much more. The messages were clear and direct from his peers. Kevin learned that they would have given him a turn. He had to learn to trust them.

Kevin was pushing up against me, embarrassed and wanting to leave the scene. "What should we do now?" I asked the group.

"He should say sorry," said Jacob.

"Okay, sorry," replied Kevin, hanging his head.

Leo suggested, "Let's put it back together and clean up." They appointed Jacob to get the janitor and his mop and ladder. The children all chipped in, and Kevin eagerly helped. They hung the bucket and soaked up the spill while discussing plans for improving the clock. Peter explained to the others the idea of making a larger hole in the bottom of the bucket. Kevin was hanging back but joined in enthusiastically now. "Yea, we can use a nail to make the hole instead of a pin. I'll get one." Kevin tore off to the hammer and nail supply and came back with a huge roofing nail. "Here," he shouted. His exaggerated enthusiasm nearly caused another accident on the way back when he bumped a table of water and paints. I let this go, one thing at a time.

"That'll make too big a hole. The water will run out too fast," said Leo anxiously, looking at me as if to say HELP, WHAT WILL HE DO NOW? Classmates found Kevin unpredictable. They also had to learn to trust him.

Kevin has always had difficulty being corrected or hearing ideas from others. But now staying with a group was beginning to mean more than pressing his point. As he felt the potential of acceptance by the group his need to be first or correct lessened. This happened in small degrees and with continual intervention.

Kevin quietly agreed and came back with a smaller nail. All were pleased this time, and the new hole was punctured. Kevin pointed out that the old hole had to be covered over. "Oh yea," agreed Jacob. Kevin felt confirmed. I left, hoping that they could peacefully resolve this dilemma. They asked Peter to borrow a patch kit from the physical education teacher who stayed to help put it on. (She had never applied a patch to a bucket before!) All four boys beamed with their accomplishment. The clock was ready to test.

Kevin came up to me later and asked, "Can we share the water clock?" I said that they could and noted his use of "we." Will he be able to share the clock *with* the others or will he take over? I refrained from talking to him about how to share.

Before lunch each day, we gather to talk about things we have been working on during the morning. Jacob, Leo, Michael, and Kevin proudly filled the water clock which hung in the center of our meeting place, and told about their revisions on the original water clock.

Jacob started, "We wanted to make the water go through faster, but not too fast."
Leo chimed in, "So we—"
"We used a biggish nail—" interrupted Kevin loudly.
Leo's face reddened, "KEVIN!" he shouted.
"Oh yea, sorry," Kevin responded. "When will it be my turn?" he asked.
"After me," and Leo continued his thought.
"That was a good idea, Kevin, to ask when your turn was coming. Does that make it easier to wait?" I praised.
"Yea, I have stuff to tell too," he replied.

When Leo finished, Kevin showed the nail they had used. Then I pointed out that Michael was still waiting for a turn. Michael appointed a timekeeper to tell us when one hour had passed so we could calibrate the receiving jar to show how much water had

> *"By this time the class knew I was helping, or training, Kevin to enter into projects and friendships appropriately."*

GOVERNORS STATE UNIVERSITY
UNIVERSITY PARK
IL 60466

127

dripped through the new hole. We estimated how much water would collect. As the meeting ended Kevin said loudly to everyone, "And if you are too rough, the strings of the clock will break and it'll make a big mess. So no fooling around near the clock."

Kevin was gaining. While I was still needed to model other ways of communicating or for help in joining classmates at a task, he could stay with a group now rather than leave in defeat. I could even remind him quietly to use the bathroom, and he took the advice without resentment.

Kevin began to unfold. He could show his feelings without fear of rejection and work with a group sometimes without disaster. Knowing I cared, regardless of his errors, made all the difference. He did not have to be first or right every time any more. He was learning other ways to succeed. Kevin was unusually bright and sometimes could not help but shout out his observations. He seemed to make connections before anyone else. However, his need to show this decreased as he learned to trust me and his peers. He realized he could always talk with me privately and explain his answers or thoughts then.

Self-esteem and social-skill building is laborious. It happens over years with endless reinforcement and reminding. It is a much slower process than acquisition of math facts or writing skills. The advances are harder to see. I am glad Kevin and I had the time to notice the gains and celebrate them with the class. It was a learning experience for everyone.

Some children with less severe social needs than Kevin, but needing occasional reminding, learned through observation. They heard the phrases I modeled for Kevin and I began to hear others using them. Some children learned how to help Kevin with his frustration and became skilled negotiators and mediators. Everyone in the room could see I valued Kevin as much as anyone else, despite difficult episodes. This established a tone of fairness and trust that pervaded interactions throughout the room. The children came to appreciate Kevin and learned patience and forgiveness with one another.

One day near the end of our first year together Kevin's father came to pick Kevin up and poked his head in the door. "I don't know what Kevin will do without school this summer. He's had a great year." I was astounded. It *had* been a great year in my mind, but it had not been easy. Kevin and I had come to heads more than once. The growth was subtle. I was surprised anyone else had noticed. I knew next year would help solidify Kevin's progress. I asked his father in what way the year was good for Kevin and he said that Kevin loved school, and talked about friends now—this was all new.

> *"The children came to appreciate Kevin and learned patience and forgiveness with one another."*

Chapter 10

Justine O'Keefe

Williston Central School
Williston, Vermont

Open is a Four-Letter Word

Before I was a teacher I was a bank teller employed in the main branch of a large city bank. The building was imposing: thick marble columns reaching to a vaulted ornate ceiling, rows of mahogany desks, revolving doors that protected the hushed atmosphere within from the tumult of the busy street.

From nine to three I stood in my teller's cage cashing checks, handling deposits and withdrawals, clipping Christmas Club coupons, and dealing with vast numbers of people over the touchy subject of money. At closing time I attempted to balance my cash drawer. Often this took several hours and seriously tried the patience of my supervisor. Clearly, banking was not my vocation.

After about a year of this work I read, quite by chance, A.S. Neill's *Summerhill*. I was profoundly moved by the author's vision of schooling. Here was a teacher who believed in the natural inclination of children to learn and to take responsibility for that learning. Here was a teacher who trusted children to exercise self-control and who was rewarded for that trust. I was astonished and intrigued that what one did in school could be meaningful, experiential, and related to its function in the real world.

Nothing in my own school experience had prepared me for this view of education. To me, school was round robin reading in groups labeled first, second, third, endless pages of borrowing and carrying, test papers returned face down on the desk, unvarying routines performed in enforced silence. The two years I spent in college were materially no different. Indeed, my inability to become inspired by or attracted to a course of study had resulted in my daily incarceration in the teller's cage.

I knew learning could be enjoyable; learning to read on my grandmother's knee had taught me that. I wondered what it would be like to be in a classroom where children were free to make choices, talk to one another, work with their hands, and be supported no matter what their academic abilities. I wondered how learning in cooperation with others rather than in competition with them would influence one's confidence and self-esteem. I wondered how it would feel to provide children with an education that treated them with dignity and fostered their desire to learn. To satisfy the wonderings, I decided to become a teacher.

When I re-entered college soon after, it was at the height of the Open Education Movement. In my methods courses we were lectured about hands-on science and the integrated day. We discussed meeting the needs of disadvantaged children and answered test questions about fostering self-esteem. This was teaching of the "Don't do as I do, do as I say" variety, but I was magnanimous. In a few months I'd be able to do it my way.

Like most beginning teachers, I had little to recommend me for the task ahead but enthusiasm, energy, and a desire to do well. Academically, I was ill equipped. My language skills were adequate, but I didn't know anything about teaching children to read. My foundation in math and science was weak. But my vision was strong, and through a series of fortuitous circumstances I began work in a school that was everything I had hoped for.

A Teaching Apprenticeship

I was hired as an assistant teacher. At the time, there was an excess of teachers and this was common practice. Inexperienced, certified teachers were paid inadequate wages in return for the privilege of working with a master teacher and the possibility of a full teaching position the following year. This arrangement provided me with the opportunity to be immersed in classroom life and the luxury of taking on academic and management responsibilities as I felt ready for them. I think of it now as an apprenticeship—the fifth, and most valuable year of my teacher training.

I don't know how many teachers look back on their first day as one of the happiest they can remember, but I do. Our small rural school, surrounded by the Green Mountains, overlooked a corn field and meandering river. The day was bright and warm with the crisp smell of oncoming fall. Having just moved from an industrial city in Connecticut, I felt overwhelmed by the beauty of the setting and the fulfillment of my long-time wish to be a teacher in Vermont.

Gretchen, my master teacher, and I stood at the classroom door and greeted the children as they arrived. Vickie in her red dress and shoes. Maureen with the impossibly dainty feet. Sulky Kurt. Affable Charlie. The demure and beautiful Anne. They were the veterans, the children who were returning to first, second, and third grade. The kindergartners were as new to the school as I was. We were beginning our careers together.

Later as I stood outside watching the children at play, Gretchen joined me. "Well, what do you think?" she asked. I thought about the relaxed, natural involvement of the children as they went about their morning's work, the easy interchange between adult and child, the wonder of the five year olds and the sophistication of the older children.

"It's perfect," I said. And for me it was.

That day was perfect, but many that followed were not. As was common with schools that experimented with the Open Education approach, too much had been done too soon. Connecting archways had been created to join all the classrooms, self-contained grades were eliminated and two multiage units formed, textbooks were abandoned.

These material changes were easy to make. Changing the long time practices of teachers and the responses of children were much more difficult. For many schools, such changes proved impossible. Many educators lacked the commitment, understanding, and follow-through necessary to make schools places where children were actively engaged in the business of learning.

I visited a district in northern New England and was shown several of their new elementary schools. The superintendent informed me that the schools were "open," built without internal walls. The teachers in these schools divided the open space with bookcases and file cabinets and went about their academic programs as usual. They made no changes in their traditional methods or in their approach to meet the affective needs of their students.

Such ridiculous and blatant abuses of the Open Classroom concept led educators to say, "We tried that and it didn't work." In reality they didn't try and their failures were blamed on Open Education.

But schools needed to change. They needed to become more interesting, challenging, and humane. In order to make those changes educators had a lot to learn. Learning takes time and a willingness to make mistakes, reflect on those mistakes, and try again. Moreover, it requires a belief that what one sets out to learn is important and worth the effort.

My colleagues and I believed our children were worth the effort. We agreed that the fundamentals of language and math, the basics, were only the beginning of education. The important thing

"I wondered how learning in cooperation with others rather than in competition with them would influence one's confidence and self-esteem."

131

was that children become learners. To do that they needed to think, question, experiment, and be committed to the task at hand. They needed to develop the self-confidence to take risks and to trust their own ideas and opinions. They weren't going to learn these things filling in the blanks in a workbook or memorizing their times tables. As their teachers it was our responsibility to develop a program that would help them learn to learn.

The days that followed that perfect first one were days of reconstruction. The school was still rocking from the elimination of commercial instructional programs and self-contained grades. The old structures had been torn down and replaced by urgent questions.

What curriculum and methods would replace those of basals and workbooks? How could we develop meaningful activities to engage the children academically and be accountable for who had done what and how? How could we make science more than a collection of dry leaves and seashells displayed with a magnifying glass? And what accommodations could we make for our older children who, used to traditional methods, were behaving like French peasants after the storming of the Bastille? Thorny problems like these made a lot of teachers scurry back to the safety of "chalk and talk, drill and kill."

Turning the Vision into Reality

Our strong belief in the desire of children to learn and our ability to facilitate that learning made us face those problems and seek solutions. We worked as a team, supporting one another, making suggestions, and making mistakes. In spite of the obvious chaos, children were reading, writing, and developing mathematical understandings. The positive interactions and cognitive and emotional growth demonstrated among children in our multiage classrooms convinced us that what we were trying to do was possible.

Slowly we began to develop structures and routines to ensure that each child's academic, emotional, and social needs were addressed. Each teacher became responsible for a particular group of children in kindergarten through third grade. We called these family groups because we thought of them as families within the larger community of the primary unit. These smaller groups provided a sense of intimacy and belonging; an opportunity for adult and child to develop and maintain a relationship that spanned the primary years.

They were also a home base. The children were free to move among our three rooms and engage in the activities offered in them. After constructing in the block area, role playing in the housekeeping corner, or exploring at the sand table, children returned to their family group classrooms. Teachers planned language arts and math activities for the children of their family group, met with them for

"How could we develop meaningful activities to engage the children academically and be accountable for who had done what and how? "

sharing circle and discussions, and communicated with their parents.

In the afternoons we conducted social studies and science workshops. Children engaged in the activity of their choice, thus providing an opportunity for teachers and students to work with people outside their particular family group. Later we began to employ themes as a way to organize the presentation of content and integrate academic disciplines. With an overall topic from which to draw, our planning became more focused and our instruction had greater depth. We were able to offer children a wide variety of projects from which to choose, thereby better meeting their academic and developmental needs.

Establishing regular daily and weekly routines provided the structure necessary for effective planning. The children learned the routines and took responsibility for organizing their work to best meet their personal learning styles. Because of our multiage groups, new students quickly learned the routines from those students returning for a second and third year. This greatly facilitated the often painful and slow adjustments felt by teachers and students at the onset of a new school year.

Because we used the money previously spent on workbooks and basals to provide additional resources to our school library, we were able to teach academic content through trade books and related projects. The children researched theme topics, kept notes in blank books, and created accompanying dioramas, sculptures, models, or collages.

For math instruction we used manipulatives and task cards. Each child had a folder or blank book in which to record his or her answers. We also taught math themes in patterns, capacity and volume, linear measurement, and telling time. We stressed the importance of conceptual knowledge, but lacked the experience with manipulatives to employ them fully. We often reverted to traditional drill and practice to teach arithmetic.

I struggled with math no less as a teacher than I had as a student. Through working with manipulatives and seeking ways to demonstrate and explain concepts to children, I began to improve my own understanding of the subject. After countless math lessons, two years of algebra, and a college course for elementary teachers, I finally learned place value by bundling popsicle sticks into tens with my six and seven year olds. I knew that if I was learning, the children were learning too. I became convinced that proper use of manipulatives was the key to improved math instruction, and I began to work toward that goal. Those were years of tremendous growth for all of us—teachers and students. The children grew cognitively and emotionally as children are wont to do. Further, they did so in an atmosphere that fostered their self-esteem and a sense that they shared in the education of their peers. Our class-

"Our classrooms were characterized by a spirit of cooperation and a respect for the diversity of a wide range of ages and abilities."

rooms were characterized by a spirit of cooperation and a respect for the diversity of a wide range of ages and abilities.

As educators we learned to provide open-ended activities that addressed the individual abilities of each child. We maintained a structure within which children could exercise self-control and take responsibility for their learning. And we had the satisfaction of knowing that the problems we faced in developing our program were gradually being solved.

While we were creating and refining our open approach to education, other teachers were becoming convinced it couldn't work. While our children were developing their language, reasoning, and social skills through inquiry and hands-on experience, others were marching back to basics. The term Open Education became a pejorative. Open classrooms were thought of as unstructured places where children failed to learn the basics. Test scores were down, parents unhappy, and children undisciplined. The movement to change the education of our children never materialized. Another attempt to improve our schools had failed.

I still think of mine as an open classroom. It's a little old fashioned, perhaps, but I continue to believe in the importance of being open as an educator and as a learner. To me, Open Education means thinking of curriculum as flexible enough to include a study of rocks if that's what my children really want to do or to change my plans if Russell's mother brings her mynah birds to school. It means asking questions that have several answers and talking openly about sensitive issues. It means that open acceptance of individual strengths and needs and the recognition that our differences and similarities contribute in equal measure to the richness of our lives. To me an open classroom is one in which it is safe to be and to come to know the person you really are.

Longtime Companions

- *continuity*
- *classroom community*
- *teacher as learner*
- *respect for the child as learner*
- *deep learning*
- *valuing different learning styles*
- *special needs*

In a multiage classroom June isn't the end of the year, it is merely a change of scene. It is a time for children to continue to grow physically and developmentally, for teachers to reflect and plan, and for everyone to feel secure in knowing that the relationships of the past school year will be continued and enhanced in the next. The beauty of a multiage classroom is that learning is long. Instead of months, teachers and learners have years to know one another, to develop skills, and to use them to acquire knowledge. Continuity over time is the greatest strength of the multiage classroom.

The gift of time that a multiage setting gives to those involved encourages the development of deep and lasting friendships. Often these friendships span age and grade levels and form to meet the particular needs of individuals. Such a friendship between Michael and Nick enhanced not only their lives, but our entire classroom community.

Michael had been a first grader in my one-two combination. An exceptionally bright and sensitive child, his interests and abilities set him apart from the other boys in the group. The complexity of his thoughts and his advanced cognitive development left him no one with whom to share his intellectual pursuits.

The following year Nick entered first grade. He had begun reading before the age of three, possessed advanced grammatical and spelling skills, and shared Michael's interest in and knowledge of computers. The two boys became immediate friends.

Their intellectual compatibility was obvious. They were constantly hatching schemes for building projects, creating and solving puzzles, sharing information from books, charts, and graphs. Together they were the indisputable computer trouble shooters. We all went to them with our computer questions. If they couldn't answer them they called the technology teacher for advice, carried out his instructions and got us up and running again.

Their friendship extended well beyond intellectual compatibility, however. Like many children whose cognitive development is far ahead of their emotional development, Nick had difficulty performing routine tasks necessary to function effectively in school: tying his shoes, locating his lunch box, keeping track of the daily schedule. Michael could relate to these difficulties, he had experienced many of them the year before. With a year's maturity to his credit, he was able, with obvious satisfaction, to help Nick learn to cope with the rigors of the institution.

135

The friendship Nick and Michael shared provided them both with intellectual stimulation. The personal support of his friend helped Nick adjust to the demands of schedules, keep track of his belongings, and feel more secure in the group. And Michael learned to be a leader by taking responsibility for his young friend.

As a class we benefited from the fine academic resources provided by Michael and Nick. Because the boys decided together what they wanted to learn and came to me with a plan, I was better able to meet the challenge of their formidable intellects. Walking hand in hand to the library or heads bent over blueprints for their dream house, their friendship was a model of cooperation, caring, and mutual respect. It was an invaluable model that touched us all, one that wouldn't have been possible had first-grader Nick and second-grader Michael been in single-grade classrooms.

Developing Relationships

"I believe that the secret of effectively managing the behavior and academic growth of children is to know them inside and out."

I believe that the secret of effectively managing the behavior and academic growth of children is to know them inside and out. For me, it isn't enough to know children's reading levels, math skills, or what last year's teachers thought of them. I want to know how they spend their free time, what their favorite foods and colors are, what their dog did yesterday. I want to know who they are so that I can address my teaching to that person. And I want to be known by them in similar ways.

The children with whom I work know who I am. They know I'm a fan of Charles Dickens, Chinese food, and my golden retriever. They know I can't abide sloppy work carelessly done and that I hate the color orange. They understand my style, my expectations, my sense of humor. And when I point to the door, they know they have exceeded the bounds of acceptable behavior.

My knowledge of them is no less intimate. I have witnessed the tremendous developmental changes they have experienced from age six to eight or nine. More important to them, I notice their new sneakers, ask about the progress of their loose teeth, and know whose grandma is visiting from Florida. I know when to accept a piece of work as the child's best, when to press for improvement, and when to insist that another try is necessary.

I come to know those children who would walk the plank for praise and those who are embarrassed by such demonstrations. I work closely with parents whose children have particular emotional or social difficulties. Over time, they come to trust my commitment to their children's welfare, resulting in honest communication about their problems.

The deep mutual understanding I share with my students allows us to deal straight forwardly with social and emotional issues. It also greatly facilitates my ability to provide the academic challenges appropriate to individual needs and abilities.

Because of their extended time together, members of a multiage class share a history. Just as old friends get together to reminisce about old times, children in multiage classrooms remind one another of past projects and field trips or students who have moved away. The cohesiveness of the group is enhanced by these memories of shared experiences and feelings.

With the overlap of children from class to class, the years run together for me. I often have to consult the older members of the group to clarify confusions I have about things we've done and places we've been. Not long ago, I was both chagrined and enlightened by an incident that evolved from our shared history.

A Shared History

A technology conference for the intermediate and middle school children was being held in the late spring. There was room for a few members of each third grade to be chosen by their teacher. I selected Ben and Mara. They used the computer often, but more important, were confident socially. I knew they would not be intimidated by the large numbers of older children attending the conference.

At dismissal time, I was talking informally with them about their reaction to the experience. James, a close friend of Ben's, was listening near by. A shy, quiet child he was often on the periphery of discussions and activities. In our three years together I had found that he preferred watching to participating.

Ben and Mara got in line. James, always choosing to be last, took his place. I was standing near him, picking up stray items in the coat closet. Squaring his shoulders and looking directly at me he said, "Ms. O'Keefe, how come you never pick me to go to special things? Ben always gets to go."

I was stunned. I wasn't aware that I had been partial to Ben and unfair to James. "What do you mean?" I asked.

James reminded me of two previous instances, once when he was six and the other when he was seven, when I had chosen Ben for participation in activities to which a limited number of children were invited. By the clarity of his answer I knew he had given the matter careful thought. He had me. My bruised teacher ego lay deflated at his feet.

"Well, James," I said, "you're right about those times. I'd forgotten about them. I'm sorry. I didn't mean to be unfair."

I explained that I didn't choose him because I didn't think he liked unfamiliar situations with large numbers of people he didn't know. I thought he'd be uncomfortable, that he wouldn't want to go. The look of understanding that crossed his face told me I hadn't been entirely wrong.

"Gee, James. I'm sorry. I made a mistake and it's too late to make it up to you."

"The experience strengthened our friendship and helped each of us to come to know ourselves better."

137

He shrugged and smiled. "It's OK. I know you didn't mean it," he said as the line filed out to the buses.

At first, I could only think that James's memory of our time together was marred by three occasions for disappointment. I felt remiss. As I thought further about it I realized that something more than disappointment had made James speak up.

During our years together James had grown comfortable in our classroom environment. He had been encouraged to take risks and had been rewarded for them. His fragile self-confidence began to strengthen. It had taken three years and as many disappointments before James trusted me enough to point out my injustice to him.

Our shared history had taught us both important lessons. In the future I'll be more careful selecting children for special activities. Hopefully, James will continue to speak up for himself and avoid similar disappointments. The experience strengthened our friendship and helped each of us to come to know ourselves better.

On the last day of school I stood outside as the children filed through the door. I said my private good-bye to each of them. I was going on sabbatical and they were off to different teachers and new classrooms the next year. James came through the door burdened with backpack, sweatshirt, lunch box, and baseball glove. He dropped everything and gave me an enthusiastic hug—a hug expressive of everything we'd been through together and all the times we'd shared.

Time is an essential element of any job well done. For me, it is the greatest benefit of a multiage classroom—time to establish deep interpersonal understandings and lasting friendships. Multiage fosters a shared history and memories that put into perspective what we've learned and who we are.

Silas's Timetable

I don't know how many times a parent has said to me as the four-year-old is wreaking havoc in the block area during our conference, "Wait 'til you get this one. He's not at all like his sister. He has no interest in letters and numbers." From experience most parents understand the vast differences that can occur between children of the same age. Hopefully, most teachers share this knowledge of child development.

Most schools, however, assume that all six-year-olds will learn in the same way, the same things, at the same speed. Hence the first-grade classroom and ten months to learn the first grade curriculum. Children who don't adhere to this timetable are often retained because they didn't move forward fast enough.

Basals divided learning to read into monthly increments. Achievement tests test reading in monthly increments. In twenty years I've never met a child who learned to read in monthly increments. Every child's timetable for learning to read is different. In a multiage classroom there is time for children to learn at their own pace, in their own style, and on their own developmental schedule.

Silas Learns to Read and Write

Several years ago I taught a self-contained kindergarten. On the first day of school I sat at a table with oak tag cards and colored markers while the children were engaged in independent activities. Individually I called children over and asked them to write their name on one of the oak tag cards. Most wrote their first name using upper case with the requisite number of letters reversed. Some wrote their first and last names. Lindsey wrote her first, middle, and last, the names of her mom and dad, her little brother, and their cat. And Silas wrote. . . .

In the ensuing weeks I observed Silas closely, trying to understand who he was and how he learned. I realized that when he wasn't greeted with an enthusiastic "Hello, Silas!" upon his arrival he was surly and distant the rest of the day. I discovered that Silas was reluctant to engage in an activity until he had had the opportunity to watch others do it. Only after he had noted the steps in the procedure and understood what was involved was he willing to give it a try. Thus, he was always among the last children to work with me on new activities.

While I was engaged with a small group of children making leaf prints, building staircases with rods, or practicing letter formation, Silas was taking note of what people were doing and saying in preparation for his turn. Usually these observations were made

"I discovered that Silas was reluctant to engage in an activity until he had had the opportunity to watch others do it."

139

covertly from his vantage point in the block area where he created and destroyed elaborate castles and ships.

As the year progressed, so did the children. They learned letter names and sounds, developed number sense, and became more adept socially. Many took the first steps in unraveling the mysteries of reading.

Consistently last, Silas practiced letter formation in sand, traced over my writing with finger and pencil, copied under a model, and finally formed his own version of S-I-L-A- and S. The process was slow and frustrating. After an intense period of concentration he would smack his pencil down on the table, push back his chair, and announce in his deep voice, "I'm done." Little by little, the S stood upright and the rest of the letters followed. Silas had learned to write his name.

Witnessing this growth was exciting and I knew there was much more to come. Perhaps I'd been a multiage teacher too long, but I felt like I was just getting to know this group of children. I wasn't ready to let go. An opening in a first/second grade combination allowed me to stay with them another year. The following year I taught a second/third. Thus, I was able to work with the majority of those children for three years.

I wasn't surprised when Lindsey began reading early in her kindergarten year. Nor was I surprised when at the end of first grade, Silas had not yet progressed beyond the pre-primer level. I wasn't particularly worried either. After all, the child still hadn't lost a tooth, and we had one more year together. I was confident that the progress he was making would continue, and that over time he would become the reader all of us wanted him to be.

Silas had slow teeth and slowly developing reading skills. But he loved books and was blessed with accommodating parents who read to him regularly. As a result, his comprehension was excellent, his ability to infer the author's meaning and draw conclusions superior to any other child's in the room. And due to his memory for detail he was a wealth of information on a variety of subjects.

For Silas, the road to reading was a rocky one. The dichotomy between his word recognition and comprehension skills was puzzling. Moreover, he appeared to learn in leaps, after which his reading became static. Those plateaus lasted several weeks, sometimes months, and caused no little concern for his parents and me. Silas was one child who refused to move smoothly from one developmental stage to the next.

Silas's timetable for learning to read was vastly different from that of his peers. He didn't master reading in monthly increments or in yearly increments either. But when he left the primary, Silas was an avid and fluent reader. He learned to read the way he learned to write his name: with careful observation and practice, performed on his own schedule, and at his own speed.

140

One Size Fits All

Sunlight pours through the windows onto our circle space where a group of young children are preparing for a chip trading lesson. They are arranging their trading boards and sorting yellow and blue chips into cardboard egg cartons. My trading board and chips are in place before the chart paper and markers.

The other children, older ones, will engage in a more advanced chip trading lesson when I have finished this one. They are ready to begin combining collections, a first step to renaming in addition and subtraction. But while I am occupied with their younger peers, they will be writing in their journals.

Upon distributing the journals, I find we don't have enough of the yellow composition books which are used for that purpose. I excuse myself and head down the hall to the teacher supply room.

When I get there I have difficulty locating the composition books. I find several stacks of them, but they are all labeled in colored marker with the names of children from other classrooms. I am aware of time going by. I keep looking.

Teachers come in and begin to converse. I am drawn into their discussion. More time goes by. I am uneasy. I know I must get back to my children with or without the journals.

I push through the group of people crowding the narrow supply room and move quickly down the dim corridor. At the door of my room I look in. The sun still illuminates the circle of math materials. Pencils, crayons, papers litter the tables. But the children are gone.

School dreams are a regular occurrence in my nocturnal life. This one, so vivid I can image it still, took place on a summer night in early July. These dreams are usually of common anxieties I experience in my life as a teacher. I'm late, not properly prepared, or the children are behaving in a way that manifests a teacher's worst fears.

Of itself, this dream was not unusual or even particularly frightening. I'm sure the children are safe. Maybe they've gone to recess or off to lunch. What struck me was the realization that the classroom about which I dream is multiage. Even in my dreams I am managing groups of learners of various ages and developmental levels.

The Tools of Learning

To some people, multiage teaching sounds more like a night-mare than a dream. The notion of teaching six, seven, and eight year

"I make the tools of learning available to children and guide them in their use."

141

olds all at the same time is as inconceivable to them as my mechanic's ability to repair my car is to me. "How do you do that?" they want to know.

I do it through open-ended activities. Tasks that engage children's hands and minds and can be tailored to individual needs, abilities, interests, and developmental levels—through school work that harnesses the energy and curiosity of children and is carried out in the active mode that is natural to them. School work that comes in enough forms to address a diversity of styles, that allows people to be challenged in those areas in which they are particularly capable, and nurtured and helped along in those they find difficult.

It is not preparing a different lesson for each child or asking children to move through the math text at their own pace. It is providing a framework within which children function as the learners they are.

I make the tools of learning available to children and guide them in their use. I give them the time and support necessary to thoroughly engage in the task at hand and trust in their intrinsic desire to learn. That is my work. The way children use the tools available to them, the degree to which they exert themselves, and the learning that results is the individual child's work.

The tools of reading are books. Fiction, nonfiction, controlled vocabulary, predictable, and wordless books are available for selection from our classroom library. During our daily half-hour of quiet reading, I listen to individuals read from books they have chosen. Either on their own or with my help, children select books at their instructional reading level.

At our conference I help the child develop his or her decoding and oral reading skills. I often listen to him or her give a retelling of a section of the book. This illustrates the child's knowledge of character, sequence, and detail. Comprehension questions check for the child's ability to make inferences, draw conclusions, and understand the main idea.

While I am thus engaged with one child, several others are practicing passages they will read during our coming conferences. Others are reading silently, to a friend, or poring over illustrations and diagrams.

On the left side of his desk, Jason makes a tidy stack of the half-dozen story books he has selected for quiet reading. He takes the book from the top of the pile, reads it, and places it on the right side of his desk. By the end of the half hour, all the books will be in the completed stack. Erika reads several chapters of her "Little House" book. Six year olds Anne and Elizabeth prefer to read together, helping one another decode words and sharing in the enjoyment of the story.

The Importance of Peer Support

Because of the wide range of abilities and ages in our multiage classroom, reading takes many forms and has many teachers. Capable readers provide a resource for figuring out difficult words. Less capable readers are supported by being read to or in having friends listen to them read. Taylor's extraordinary growth as a reader was a result of this kind of peer support.

In September Taylor was one of two five-year-olds in the class. The other child was already an accomplished reader. He read dialogue in voices and turned the page well before the beginning of the last sentence. Taylor had yet to learn the sounds and names of letters and our lengthy quiet reading period was difficult for him.

I encouraged children to read to Taylor and later to listen to him read. We started out on alphabet and predictable books and soon moved on to pre-primers.

Jeffrey and Daniel, two fellows who tended to act out, were Taylor's most dedicated teachers. They made regular reports to me about his progress and praised him highly for his efforts. Taylor was a highly motivated and willing student and his reading vastly improved. His success was matched by the enhanced self-esteem and sharpened skills of his two coaches.

Read-aloud time provides additional opportunities for children to be engaged with books. Story and chapter books entertain, sharpen children's listening skills, and provide practice in making predictions and inferences. They promote discussions of setting, time, and the motivations of the main characters. Often children whose oral reading is limited to controlled vocabulary books are adept at these high-level comprehension skills. Building on these strengths can encourage children to persevere in the difficult tasks of word recognition and decoding.

Learning to read is another tool for learning; one that spans all other disciplines. It is an especially important tool in the development of children's writing.

At regular intervals each week we hold writing workshops. Blank storybooks and journals, a variety of lined and unlined paper, and the word processor are employed at this time. Young children draw pictures and label their parts or struggle to write a related sentence. Older children begin new pieces or continue on those they have yet to complete. People who have finished a piece of writing may be correcting mechanics or working to publish it in some form. All grapple with and attempt to tame that elusive monster lurking in the sea of language known as spelling.

Process writing allows children to function at the cognitive and developmental level appropriate to them. They acquire spelling, punctuation, and grammatical skills by applying them to the real business of writing. And, most important, the content of their writing is a direct expression of their individuality.

"Because of the wide range of abilities and ages in our multiage classroom, reading takes many forms and has many teachers."

A scientist in the making, six-year-old Ben describes the cockpit of his father's small plane. He draws the instrument panel and outlines the function of each button, dial, and lever. Elizabeth's picture shows her ice skating at her grandmother's rink. From our conference I learn that she can skate backward and do a figure eight; two skills on which her younger sister Ashley is still working. Kate writes about the third tooth she has lost during circle time this year. She describes the applause of the class and the sealed envelope labeled "Kate's tooth" in which she brings the tooth home. As the blank books fill up and the writing folder becomes stuffed with crinkled and folded paper, a portrait of the inner child emerges. The interests, personal style, and written language development of each individual are graphically revealed.

During writing workshop, I listen to children read their pieces and conference with them about the next step. I sit with the younger ones and exaggerate each sound in the word they are attempting to spell. I talk to an older child about the proper use of quotation marks in the dialogue she has written. But I am not the only person performing these tasks. Children read their work to each other, help with spelling, and carry on pre-writing conversations.

At circle time a particular author reads his or her piece to the class and asks for questions and suggestions. A published piece is read and placed in the classroom library or everyone has a chance to share their Monday journal entry.

At other times, children write about math discoveries, take notes on nonfiction reading related to themes, or write thank you notes after a field trip. Like reading, writing spans all curriculum areas and is a tool for learning.

Learning Math Concepts

Near the block area two sets of storage shelves house a variety of cubes, chips, rods, sticks, geoboards, and pattern blocks. They are sorted into labeled, kid-proof containers and are the tools of our mathematics program. Behind these shelves, there are large laminated pieces of oak tag, math mats for each child labeled with his or her name. The mats function both as a place on which to build and as a way to display what has been created. There is also a small basket that holds the blank books in which the children record their written math work.

I teach certain math concepts as integrated units: time, money, measurement, geometry. We study the history of calendars and clocks, design our own time pieces, create a timeline of our lives or the school year. During a money unit we learn to play a money-trading game, set up a classroom restaurant or store, perhaps visit a local bank. We discuss the development of standard units of measure after exploring the use of digits, cubits, and paces. In geometry we look for shapes and symmetry in nature, create geometric models, and learn to use a compass and straight edge. My goal is to constantly link math to the world from which it evolved.

Much of our work in mathematics is devoted to understanding patterns and operations. Using manipulatives on my math mat, I present to the whole group the assignment for the day which I call "Ways to Count." I ask, "What's a good number to count by?" "Let's count by fours," suggests Dylan. With Unifix cubes I make several groups of fours. "How many in each group?" I ask. We count together to make certain. "How many groups have I made?" We count again.

There are ten groups of four. Across the chart paper I draw ten lines. Under each line I write a number from one to ten. We fill in the table together. One group of four is four. Two groups of four is eight. Ten groups of four is forty. Then we look for patterns. Kevin notices that the numbers four, eight, two, six, and zero repeat in the one's place. We read the numbers chorally and predict what will come next.

Their task is to choose a number and make several groups of that number. As they leave the circle, they tell me their numbers and are given their math mats. Overwhelmingly, children choose a number appropriate to their academic and developmental needs. Six-year-old Sarah chooses five. Katie, soon to be eight, chooses six. Matthew wants a challenge; he'll explore twelve. Gordon, for whom math is difficult, will create an up and down staircase, counting forward to twenty and backward to one.

Parents ask me, "What if they choose something too easy? My kid's lazy. He'd pick something he already knows." This rarely happens. When it does, we negotiate. It is important to trust children's intuitive sense of what the next step is. They usually know and want to pursue it.

While the children are working to create their groups with cubes, tiles, teddies, and chips, I talk to individuals about their work. "How many groups do you have so far?" "How many cubes is that in all?" "If you decide to make ten groups, how many more will you need to make?" Children's answers help me evaluate their performance and know what they should work on next.

Because I want children to understand that the math they do with manipulatives is linked to abstract symbols, I prepare a page in their math record book similar to the table we created on the chart paper. As children finish the assignment I meet them at their math mat for a final count down.

I ask Katie to read her counting by six numbers aloud from her math book. Six, twelve, eighteen, twenty-four, thirty, thirty-six, forty-two, forty-nine. . . Oops. I ask her to look at her work and correct her mistake. With a twinkle of defiance in her eyes and a smile on her face she says, "You mean mistakes, Ms. O'Keefe. Everything after forty-nine is wrong too." She's a clever girl, that Katie,

"Much of our work in mathematics is devoted to understanding patterns and operations."

and confident too. We both know that she has the tools and skills necessary to solve her problem.

This early work in number patterns encourages children to look for other patterns in mathematics: in the hundreds board, in money counting, in multiplication. It is an example of an open-ended activity that encourages children to use the tools of mathematics to meet their diverse needs and abilities.

Meeting Individual Needs

Books, papers, pencils, and math manipulatives are important tools for learning. In addition our classroom houses a myriad of art materials: paints and brushes, inks and brayers, colored chalk, tissue, metallic, construction paper, collage materials, and rubber stamps. We use these tools of artistic expression to enhance our reading, writing, and math.

Cut paper, crayons, and paint can translate the mental images stimulated by the oral reading of a book into a visual retelling of the story. Whether it's Dorothy, Toto and friends on their way to the Emerald City or the underground world of Fantastic Mr. Fox, group mural making actively and personally involves children in the magic of literature. Illustrating with watercolors, chalk, or collage enhances the individual expression of each child's writing. Creating a pattern with rubber stamps or constructing and decorating geometric models engage children in the logic and beauty of mathematics.

"Messing about" is a natural mode of learning for young children. Art encourages them to join the abstract world of letters and numbers to the concrete experiences of painting, modeling, drawing, and building. Linking art to the three R's results in learning activities that capture the imagination, harness the energy, and express the intellects of children.

The way each child employs the tools of reading, writing, math and art reflects his or her developmental level, academic skills, and individuality. Children are able to find their places on the academic continuum and progress from there. They can take giant steps in the areas of their strengths and smaller steps in their areas of need. They can even jog in place while they work on a skill they find particularly challenging or for which they lack the necessary physical maturity or intellectual development.

Open-ended activities do not demand that children succeed or fail on the basis of their ability to find a single right answer. Instead, they demand each learner's best effort, full engagement, and personal expression. Open-ended activities require that learners bring to bear the people they are to the task at hand.

"'Messing about' is a natural mode of learning for young children."

What I Learned From the Stories

Charles Rathbone

I undertook The Writing Project for two reasons. I wanted to see if there was correspondence in the classroom organization of other multiage classroom teachers to what I observed in Room A. I also wanted to see the correspondence between Anne's treatment of cooperative learning and the treatment of cooperative learning by the writers.

The writers and I used a different language to talk about classroom practices that revealed our differing perspectives. I attributed seven elements to the Room A environment. They noted eleven characteristics that embrace similarities in their stories. We are both clear on the presence of continuity. Beyond that, there are subtle differences in what was described. The differences emerge from our perspectives as insiders (the writers) and outsider (me) and will be dealt with more fully in the next chapter.

With regard to the cooperative learning issue, none of the teachers either wrote about or talked about cooperative learning strategies and techniques directly. They were like Anne in their approach to issues of cooperation and collaboration in the classroom. Modeling cooperation, having children working together, and teaching children how to work together is so much a part of their practice that the application of a technique seems unnecessary. There seemed to be a good deal of learning cooperatively in their settings that was informally and intentionally present most of the time.

Part Three

Reflections on Multiage Teaching and Learning

This final section addresses the question of what do I make of all this? What reflections do I have about what I have seen, heard, and felt, and what conclusions can be drawn from the thoughts the five of us generated over the better part of a year?

People who conduct qualitative studies are not generally expected to create conclusions from their research. This softer qualitative effort has allowed me to show rather than tell about these multiage settings and I want to share several realizations I've had since concluding the study. My work has not stopped. I still spend time with teachers in varied settings. I still try to keep learning at the focal point of what I believe about teaching. I still seek places in schools where children can be involved in meaningful work. Having finished the study, my perspective on multiage has broadened and in turn, understandings gleaned from the study have deepened. These understandings form the structure of the final four chapters. The one commentary that is not inspired by post-study reflection is the commentary on Vygotsky and multiage. I became familiar with some of Vygotsky's writings during the study but I include it in this final section because of its direct bearing on why I believe the practices we have described are so powerful a learning environment.

Chapter 11

A Model of Multiage Teaching

When I first planned this study of multiage teaching and learning, I thought the two studies would provide distinctly different vantage points from which to look at multiage practice. They do.

In Part I, The Classroom Study, I was an involved observer who camped out in Room A, attempting to make sense of what I saw. In Part II, The Writing Study, four teachers described definitive moments in their multiage teaching and agreed on common characteristics of their practice.

But I also thought the findings would come together in a way they do not. The language of my seven elements and the teachers' eleven characteristics is different in tone and also in kind. Forcing one set of findings upon the other for some kind of grand conclusion doesn't really work. Thus, my inquiry presented me with a dilemma. If I couldn't find in the work a " Presto! Magic! Here Is *the Definitive Statement* about Multiage Practice!!!," would the description of practice and reflections on that practice be enough? Over a few months of putting the work aside, I regained my perspective on the research and realized the "Presto! Magic!" outcome wasn't what this work was all about anyway. (The old tapes of quantitative conclusion finding die hard.)

I had set out to describe the teaching and learning environment in multiage classrooms. Not all multiage classrooms. These four multiage classrooms. Remembering this purpose, a model of multiage practice that included multiple points of view began to emerge.

This model shows multiage practice from both the insider and outsider points of view. The insiders are the teachers of this study. Their vantage point is represented in the inner-most areas of the model, the areas that contain their values and dispositions. As I studied and worked with their characteristics, it became clear the

" . . . a model of multiage practice that included multiple points of view began to emerge."

149

writers had identified two categories: their core values as teachers ("What do you believe about yourself as a teacher?"); and what I would call habits of practice, a kind of disposition to teach in a certain way ("What do you do as a teacher?").

Teacher Values:

- a profound and fundamental respect for the child as learner and response to the child as a learner
- seeing self as both teacher and learner
- seeing teaching from a perspective that is embracingly holistic
- valuing different kinds of learning

Teacher Dispositions:

- planning for deep learning
- planning for spontaneity
- promoting continuity in all forms
- providing for active learning
- promoting conversation, intentional and unintentional, wherever possible
- making time open-ended
- establishing the classroom community

Graphically, the characteristics look this way and represent how the insiders in the study talk about teaching as they knew it.

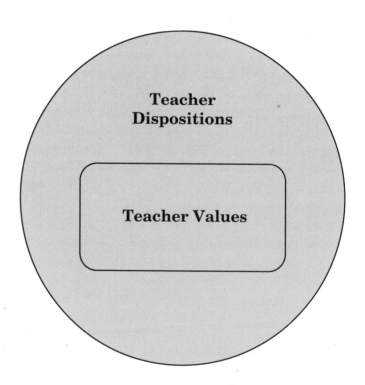

The "outsider" point of view represents what I concluded about the teaching and learning environment in Room A. I know about these kind of places, but, and it is a significant but, my knowledge is the knowledge of an outsider. I must not presume to know these settings as an insider would. The model shows this distinction.

As an outsider, I describe the classroom climate as follows:

The Teaching/Learning Climate:

- informal
- shows continuity
- has overlapping events
- shows grouping variety
- reveals a sense of family
- shows routine procedures
- shows multiple interactions

But another part of the outsider's perspective was so obvious when I first entered Room A, that I almost missed it. This perspective names what any knowledgeable teacher would see and recognize walking into a classroom as the taught curriculum.

The "Taught Classroom Curriculum" is identified by the observer, not by the person doing the teaching.

The Taught Classroom Curriculum:

- whole language
- theme units
- project work
- cooperative groupings
- play time
- manipulative math
- hands-on science
- classroom meetings

"I know about these kind of places, but, and it is a significant but, my knowledge is the knowledge of an outsider."

Overall, the model of teaching and learning in a multiage environment that emerges from this study looks like this.

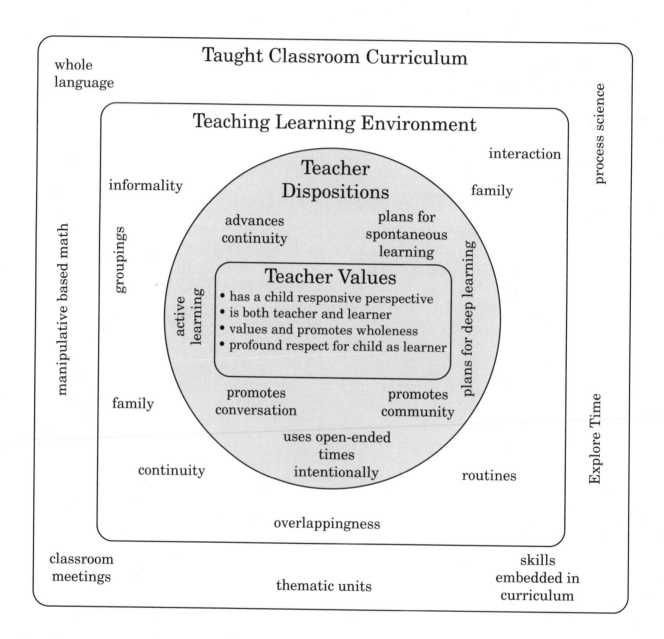

This way of thinking about multiage teaching and learning brings together the findings of the two studies in way that illuminates each of them.

Because of its inside/outside construction, the model also shows why it is two people can see the same thing and reach two rather different conclusions about what they saw. For example, an observer might conclude these were whole language classrooms or cooperative learning classrooms. I don't think any of the four teachers in the study would use these terms as an overall descriptor of her room. Yet the term might well communicate to the visitor what he or she was seeing.

It is only at the level of what is actually going on from moment to moment with the children in the classroom that the insider/outsider might actually agree on what he or she saw. That layer of experience is represented in the text of the study, not in the model.

The model also has a kind of dynamic explanatory quality to it depending upon how you choose to enter it.

From the outside in: it does signify that one can never really know what is in the mind of a teacher even though you see lots of things in her classroom that are familiar to you and that you think you know a good deal about.

From the inside out: it shows that at the heart of any teaching enterprise is a set of values. For the teachers involved in the study, values were consistent with practice. There is an evident congruence between value and disposition in the moments they chose to exemplify as the most definitive of their multiage teaching lives. The model could be used to generate discussion about times teachers feel their values and practices are congruent or in conflict.

The model also suggests that these teachers (all teachers?) are not necessarily defined by what others see in their classrooms. The reasons for why they do what they do lie more in explanation and example than in observation and conclusion drawing.

The model may also be particularly useful for readers who are considering adapting current practices (Taught Classroom Curriculum) in a single grade setting so that they might teach in a multiage setting. For example, the model depicts a responsiveness to children as learners as a core value for (these) multiage teachers. If a teacher was going to teach a thematic unit say, on water, the model gives several guidelines for teaching that unit in a way that begins to create a responsiveness to learners. Look at the dispositions noted by the multiage writers. Designing into the water unit opportunities for open-ended inquiry, highly structured at the beginning, would be one way to promote teaching success in a multiage setting. Making sure the children had time to talk and write about their work would be another. Expecting multiple outcomes rather than one particular kind of outcome would be another. Building a project that had connections with some work already accomplished would be another, and so on.

The model suggests there are many different avenues into multiage practice. The issue of becoming proficient may be more a question of values and dispositions than finding the right curriculum to use. Success lies in the adaptation of curriculum and the model begins to suggest what those avenues might be.

> *"The issue of becoming proficient may be more a question of values and dispositions than finding the right curriculum to use."*

Chapter 12

A Multiage Perspective from the Writings of Lev Vygotsky

When I was first teaching in an urban junior high school, I remember a university-based psychologist who came to our school to help us better serve our charges. David Hunt captured my attention with the idea of matching models (Hunt, 1971), the notion that you place your instructional level just ahead of a child's current independent learning level in order to motive and inspire the child's learning. He actually demonstrated ways to accomplish this end. I learned many things from him, not the least of which was how to survive in a classroom with students of highly diverse abilities and interests.

My survival in that school was the beginning of my interest in how groupings of diverse abilities could promote learning better than groupings of similar ability.

Since then, I have participated in enough heterogeneous classrooms to know that diversity, properly honed and fashioned, can create and augment a powerful learning environment for groups of learners who look very different from each other. There exists a strong research base to establish the superiority of this kind of learning for all learners in terms of attitude towards one another and academic achievement, regardless of ability or interest. What has been lacking is a strong theoretical base for how a multiage, multiability environment works to enhance and facilitate learning. The research base is strong, but it is more grounded in instructional technique than developmental theory.

The publication of Intelligence and Experience (Hunt, 1963), enabled the research of Jean Piaget to provide a theoretical base for teaching and learning that is more child-centered than teacher directed, constructive than passive, transactional than imposed. Practitioners who have been interested in a theoretical basis for their classroom work note Piaget's use of physical and social interaction as prerequisite to mental development and equate it to their activity-oriented learning strategies. Yet Piaget remains fundamentally biological in his view of learning. Beyond noting the importance of social interaction with peers and with the wisdom of the ages as other humans pass their history along to succeeding generations, there is surprisingly little in his work to support the active use of heterogeneous groupings of children as a particular benefit for learning.

A chance reference to Vygotsky's work led me to read *Mind and Society* (1978) while I was writing the initial proposal for this research. While I claim only beginner's knowledge of his work, I believe it promises strong theoretical support for learning that accrues through the use of multiage student groups in classroom settings. This promise is exciting. In many ways it confirms the wisdom of practice spoken to by the Collaborative.

Through these teachers' dispositions towards wholeness, spontaneity, activity, depth, variation of form, and community in learning, they create learning situations that are self-sustaining and motivating for all their students. What theoretical explanation is there for this success? Vygotsky provides an answer, both within his general notion of learning and in his particular formulation of "the zone of proximal development" (ZPD).

The writers identified learning by eavesdropping, priming the pump, learning by watching, and learning on the edge. None of these are terms that would hold much credibility with the conventional American norm of mastery in learning through directed teaching. The terms make sense within a Vygotskian framework.

Vygotsky writes about what children know and how they come to know what they don't know. His knowledge embraces literary narratives as well as findings from his own research. He writes about children's ability to learn something taught to them that they couldn't learn on their own. And he writes about their inability to learn other things even when it is taught to them. He notes that development gives children the ability to learn things beyond what they know if someone is able to teach it to them as they can learn it. "As they can learn it" is a critical phrase. At first, they will only be able to accomplish the learning along with their teacher. Bruner (1986) refers to the teacher's work in this instance as "scaffolding." Soon, they will be able to accomplish the task on their own, independently. Vygotsky calls this area of potential learning that soon becomes actual learning "the zone of proximal development."

"Vygotsky writes about what children know and how they come to know what they don't know."

155

It is the distance between the actual developmental level as determined by independent problem solving and the level of potential development as determined through problem solving under adult guidance with more capable peers.

We propose that an essential feature of learning is that it creates the zone of proximal development; that is, learning awakens a variety of internal developmental processes that are able to operate only when the child is interacting with people in his environment and in cooperation with his peers. Once these processes are internalized, they become part of the child's independent developmental achievement. From this point of view, learning is not development; however, properly organized learning results in mental development and sets in motion a variety of developmental processes that would be impossible apart from learning.

Vygotsky underscores the importance of the social group and the individual's interactions within the social group as more than facilitative of learning. From his point of view, learning is caused by the internalization of speech and language exercised and extended in the social group. This is quite a different emphasis from Piaget's belief that learning is primarily an internal construction.

The Collaborative writers see the social group operating in this fashion rather constantly in their classrooms. They know there are always children watching, listening, rehearsing in their minds or vicariously participating in the learning of other children. The writers see these acts of looking and listening as a kind of preparation for learning to come. The story of Mary Lou and the word-find is a wonderful example of this. There are others that happen every day. These watchers and listeners are in the zone of proximal development. They are moving from potential learning to actual learning. They are becoming accustomed to a learning that they will soon be able to evidence.

I have come to believe that Anne's room is a zone of proximal development. The multiage mix and times of overlapping activities makes so many zones available to so many children it would be impossible for a researcher to note and identify them all. When the Collaborative writers speak of children helping each other as a natural occurrence in their rooms, they underscore the fact that their teaching is oriented towards making this zone as rich as possible. Their achieving the proper balance of children in their rooms is their way of creating the best possible zone for potential learning. The conversation and activity they intentionally promote "presupposes a specific social nature and process by which children grow into the intellectual life of those around them."

Cooperation seems essential.

What the child can do in cooperation today he can do alone tomorrow. Therefore, the only good kind of instruction is that which marches ahead of development and leads it; it must be aimed not so much at the ripe as at the ripening functions. [With other methods of instruction] in offering the child problems he was able to handle without help, this method failed to utilize the zone of proximal development and to lead the child to what he could not yet do. Instruction was oriented to the child's weakness rather than his strength, thus encouraging him to remain at the preschool stage of development (Vygotsky 1986).

Because learning "presupposes a specific social event," Vygotsky (1978) underscores the importance of speech in a young child's learning. He sees speech as equally as important as activity.

The Collaborative writers know through the wisdom of practice that conversation and interaction are strong elements of their class-rooms. Their practice is entirely compatible with Vygotsky's thought. At one point in our conversations the writers wanted to label their conversation category, "Talk, Talk, And More Talk." But we knew it wasn't only talk that created the situations of learning. These teachers met usually three or four times a day with their children in circle time to introduce new learnings and to recall and analyze learnings just accomplished. The reviews are done in the class with children of varied ages participating.

I have found no counter example in my reading of Vygotsky to suggest these classrooms are other than close to what Vygotsky would prescribe as an appropriate setting for learning. Usually, older children provide a model of learning just ahead of the younger. Sometimes, it is the younger who provide the model. Children feel comfortable to sit in on other children's learnings because of the informal nature of the setting. Thematic study and project work that is generated from curiosities expressed by the children ensure that work in progress is interesting stuff for the children. The interaction and conversation about what occurs links thought, action, and intellectual development.

The elements of multiage teaching and learning identified in the study of Room A and the writers' classrooms are compatible with the view of learning proposed by Vygotsky. Most telling is the match of informal language used by the teachers and the quite formal criteria used by Vygotsky for appropriate settings. Seventy years and unknown cultural differences define the vast difference between the Russian thinker and the Vermont practitioners. What unites them are their careful eyes and thoughtful reflections about the one universal that forms their bond: how children gather meaning from their world.

"What the child can do in cooperation today he can do alone tomorrow."

Chapter 13

Researcher Bias: A Comment on Folder Scribbling.

I began this research so I could describe the teaching and learning environment of a multiage classroom. Yet my affirmation lacks conviction some days because the research keeps nudging my thinking. It is unsettled and it seems undone. However, I have confidence that what I learned will be useful to others who are themselves curious about how learning occurs in settings where diversity is intentionally maximized.

I am aware that my professional history with multiage teaching and learning could have influenced my thinking in conducting these studies. In at least one instance it did and I'd like to show how it occurred. I carried out this research because I've spent a professional lifetime simply fascinated with the notion that multiage classrooms are better environments for children's learning. A journal entry prior to the beginning of the field work puts my bias squarely on the table.

> I have this thing about multiage class settings. Not just rooms filled with children of different ages placed there deliberately — one could still have all the fives in one section and all the sixes in another. For me, multiage is a set of dispositions to teach in the richest way possible, to teach in a way that embodies the deep interests of children, to teach in a way that makes possible the natural movement of children to the edges of what they know and beyond until new information out there becomes part of the known, part of their working knowledge structures. It is evolutionary for their learning structures, often revolutionary for the child. It is always active, physically or otherwise, it is sometimes contemplative, passive and perhaps even dreamy. It is not on the whole

preordained, imposed, sequential. And it can be bits and pieces of all these.

But why the fascination? To be absolutely truthful, I'm not really sure. My intuition, my feelings tell me that the multiage settings I see that resonate with my beliefs about the way the world should be are simply right. Just that. Simply right. Great research-able term, "right."

In them I see children cooperating and building internal structures and external realities together. I see teachers as facilita-tors of that process, but facilitation is such a limp term. They are also seducers and manipulators of the first order, intuitively con-trolling the physical and material elements of the classroom setting so as to enable real questions to appear and be pursued. And I see much of what the traditionalists would call disorder. Children at work supposedly, talking about one or several things while doing quite another. Cues coming from many sources around a room, distractions too. It's all part of the mix. Things get worked on, put away, brought out again, revised, elaborated, corrected, perhaps discarded, perhaps finished. There is talk, often much talk, some of it directed to task. And there is hearing and there is listening. In the listening is the potential connection that bridges the present piece to the future piece. It can come from anywhere. Most often it comes from another child who sees from having been there once before , not too long ago, who perhaps unknowingly or even very know-ingly makes the useful statement that is really heard.

My advocacy of these proper settings derives from rather straight-forward thoughts. The world is multiage, why not schools? Learning is building from within, why not encourage the construc-tion? Boys are at risk in silent places, why not free them a bit? Early competition for someone else's prize segregates winners and los-ers. Why not delay this sorting to its more proper time (if in fact there ever is one)? We are whole entities we human beings, why not school us so as to use all our strengths, individually and collec-tively? Knowledge is gained through continued human interac-tions, why not create proper social environments for this to hap-pen? To fail is only another part of the learning cycle, why not create settings where it really is okay to fail and to understand? Teaching must model learning, why not regard teachers as learners?

So all this is why I want to look at the learning that goes on in multiage groups and why I'm curious about children's perspective on this learning. I am driven to know more about these two areas. I am equally driven to want others know more about them. My overall goal I suppose is to assemble a series of documents and artifacts that clarify learning in a multiage world. It is not my intent to confuse skeptics with information; merely to provide those of well-intentioned curiosity with good information—visual, verbal, and print.

Because of this fascination, I want to know more about these settings. I have moved in and out of these settings like a humming-bird, drinking deeply from the richness each had to offer but staying only momentarily to accomplish my ends. I had never lived in one for any length of time. My bias made my looking sharper and I believe more focused. I was a tougher observer. But I also carried a

"For me, multiage is a set of dispositions to teach in the richest way possible"

preconception of an essential goodness to these settings. This became inappropriate in at least one instance during the study, my viewing of misbehavior in the afternoons.

During the times Anne would be working with smaller groups of students, I was free to watch what the other children were doing. From my point of view, there was too much silliness and fooling around. I saw the children scribbling in their work folders and I was bothered by this wanton destruction.

opposing

"I was a tougher observer. But I also carried a preconception of an essential goodness to these settings."

> They mark and deface their folders. It is interesting to watch. It's almost as if it is just something to do. "We'll draw on the folders, scribble, sharpen our leads on them, poke holes in them." I wonder if this behavior gets more intense because the morning is so much more active. The more passive afternoon activity may be felt all the more by the kids and they are taking it out on their folders.

> At the same time I was struggling to understand it.

> I also just have to wonder if the afternoon peskiness that I call "misbehavior" is only that in my eyes. Anne may see it as something else, an inevitable result of kids being more tired in the afternoon. . . .

Several months later, I was observing children in another multiage room in another school.

> On Thursday, I noticed a lot of the same scratching in Marni's room, especially with a group of boys who were writing in each other's presence and sharing what they had written with one another. I was astonished to see the same pattern of destruction (my word now) as I had seen in Anne's room.

I felt like carrying out another separate research project on doodling, a term somewhat more peaceful than folder destruction! What I noticed at this other school gave me a different perspective on scribbling and I began to put the misbehavior issue to rest.

> Clearly the judgment is a manifestation of my value system, my mind, my sensitivities. Some kids deface folders willfully as a destructive act. Some kids deface folders as a way to keep engaged with a path of thought while they are thinking. Some defacement is figuring things out and is not defacing at all in the willful sense. Some kids just scribble without thought at all. Some kids deface as a contest with other kids. For others it is just a game. Some kids do all of the above. So what? Good question! For me it was important. For Anne, it was part of the turf.

Anne was real clear about its importance.

> Well, if I had to think about major things that went on in the room, folder defacing wouldn't be one of them. It wasn't anything

I would spend much time on. There are far more important things to concentrate on, like working with those small groups. I guess there are trade-offs. Sure I'm aware these things go on. But my first attention must be to the kids I am working with and I don't want to interrupt important works with them when something significant is going on. I give them my full attention. Just to quiet someone else down isn't worth it most of the time. There has to be some misbehavior. If there weren't, it wouldn't be real.

One reason I think it is harder to teach in this more informal setting is the lack of clarity between acceptable and unacceptable behavior. It is a thin line sometimes. I always have to be aware of what the kids are doing in order to help them back over the line if they cross it. That takes a lot of energy, more energy than a formal, strict setting. In that setting, the major thread is control, not learning.

I realized that being an involved observer didn't necessarily mean I was a better observer. I was uncomfortable with the misbehavior I saw because I had a stake in Room A being a place of positive working conditions. It took a long time to recognize the judgment I was making (scribbling, folder destruction) was affecting my observation. Working through the preconceptions I brought to this familiar terrain made my observational process clearer.

Chapter 14

Answers to the Most Frequently Asked Questions About Multiage Teaching and Learning

I am asked lots of questions about multiage classrooms in my professional life. These studies have given me an additional perspective on some of these questions and I thought it might be useful to deal with several in this concluding chapter.

Q: Have things changed at the school since your residency?

A: The research was carried out in the spring of 1990. Since then, change has continued at Shelburne. When one Multiage team member retired at the end of the 1990 school year, a colleague and close friend to Anne, a teacher with whom she shared a classroom wall, joined the Multiage team. Her transition was quite seamless. The village finally did pass a bond issue supporting the construction of a new elementary school, the construction to be added to the newer middle school. Preliminary plans suggest a form of construction conducive to teaming and multiage configurations.

Anne Bingham retired at the end of the 1993 school year and is to be replaced by the first male multiage teacher ever to serve at the Village School. Anne is contemplating writing a book, a multiage manual.

The Multiage team now has a name, "Explorers."

The teachers of the specials have begun to work with multiage groupings.

And finally, I was invited to the school and asked to present our findings shortly after my residency was completed. Although the analysis was very much still in process, our discussion reflected an informed professional dialogue on the most basic issues of teaching and learning, a discussion multiage seems to provoke in many places. Change in Multiage continues to be part of its fabric. And the model of teaching and learning it proposes has clearly had an effect on the schooling discussions and decision making of its affiliated communities.

Q: How does increasing classroom diversity lead to enhanced learning opportunities?

A: Teachers who struggle to meet all the needs of their children in conventional classrooms cannot comprehend how they could possibly do more in a classroom that is even more diverse. The notion of increasing the diversity in their classrooms seems absolutely irresponsible to them. The writers' message is that it is accomplished by teachers taking a different kind of responsibility for their children's learning. They turn more learning responsibility over to their children and they ensure that the opportunities and models are present. What they guarantee in this exchange is that they the teachers will have interesting things to pursue in the classroom and the children will have some choice in what is to be learned. The children also have lots of different models for going about their learning because of the mix of children in the classroom. They've given children things to learn that are valued in the children's eyes and have done so in a manner that ensures a reasonable amount of success. In short, they've built a classroom environment that creates intrinsic motivation. And they've made sure there are plenty of opportunities for the children to learn from each other in a predictable classroom setting. They carry checklists of required skills and content in their heads and record progress notes on clipboards kept on their desks or placed in strategic locations throughout their rooms. They keep an eye on what their children know academically. One way or another, whether it's over a one-year period or a four-year period, the "have to's" are addressed. They are taught (or learned) as a consequence of children's learning interesting stuff. The increased time with one teacher means time has become variable and learning is more of a constant. Graded settings seem to make time constant and learning variable.

"They turn more learning responsibility over to their children and they ensure that the opportunities and models are present."

Q: Why did the multiage classrooms you studied have such a powerful reputation for a certain kind of learning?

A: Anne, her students, other teachers in the school, parents in the larger community, and the writers all have a certain kind of classroom environment in mind when they think of multiage. The times of the classroom day the children experience most intensely are the times when the characteristic elements that surfaced in the classroom study are most apparent. Therefore, regardless of what occurs at other times during the day, the classroom environment of the multiage setting is typified by the elements of informality, grouping, interaction, and so on.

Figure 4 portrays this relationship. The seven elements occur vertically; the classroom schedule occurs horizontally. In their intersection I have noted the relative intensity of occurrence for each element in each time period of Anne's day. I made the judgment simply on the basis of my experience in the classroom. Every morning sets not only the tone for the day but for the classroom setting in general. Morning holds the highest concentration of continuity, family, interaction, and informality. It is the density of these elements in the morning hours that gives Multiage, as a whole, its overall reputation.

Figure 4

Presence and Intensity of the Elements of Multiage Teaching and Learning in Room A on a Typical Day

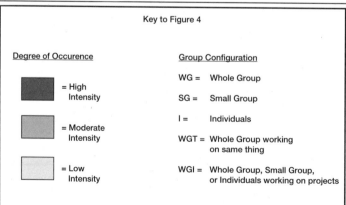

164

Q: Didn't the schools the writers taught in affect the study?

A.: Sure. Structurally, the settings represented by the writers were well-established. The writers were in a school that supported their work, although Peggy had just recently achieved that status in her new setting. Thus, they are writing from a perspective of acceptance and the momentum of success in what they do. Their stories are not the stories of starting up. They don't write about getting a multiage classroom started and what the first few years are like. Their stories are stories of classrooms well under way.

Q: Why the difference between learning cooperatively and cooperative learning?

A: History and expertise. The teachers, though they would cringe at the term, are probably what Dreyfus & Dreyfus (1980) would call "experts." This fact and their dispositions to teach in a certain way explain the difference. The writers have years of experience teaching mixed-ability groupings. They use phrases with one another that each understood immediately and that left me baffled. Planned spontaneity was one of them. Flexible structure, another. They have refined their art through conscious reflection on their practice, their teaching appears smooth and natural, they operate strongly out of principle, and they feel their imperfections dearly. These are all attributes of an expert. Thus the writings about their work is different than writings would be from the perspective of a less experienced teacher learning the craft. It is, for example, much less procedural and much more intuitive. It is natural they avoid prescriptive forms of cooperative learning and peer tutoring. They believe they accomplish the same ends without being formula-istic.

Q: Are any parts of the daily schedule absolutely necessary for multiage groupings to work?

A: Meeting times and Explore Time. Meeting times are where intentional talk serves both academic and community building purposes. Academically, the modeling of investigations and the talk about what has been learned serves to extend what groups and individuals have learned and the way they have learned it. The support children give each other during these times establishes a basic comfort for academic risk taking later on.

Anne and her team say the fifty minutes that constitute Explore Time are the most important fifty minutes of the day. Keeping that time as an uninterrupted block of time has been difficult. Mostly, they've been successful, although less time is spent in Explore Time now than when the program started.

"Their stories are stories of classrooms well under way."

They talked about time during the team interview. Their voices overlap. They interrupt each other's sentences and finish each others thoughts. In another setting, the behavior might be rude. Here, it is how it is. This is the way it has been with this team that has been together for eighteen years. They talk almost as one.

"Now another thing that has happened and I don't know what it is, something has happened with the time. We don't have as much time as we used to. We seemed to lose it and I don't know where the difference lies but somehow, things have been pushed together so that there's less. I think it's that we feel that we have more expected of us and that we have more to squeeze into the same piece of time."

Explore Time has held out despite denser curriculum requirements, invocations for new curricula (Drug and Alcohol Education, spelling programs), fewer parent volunteers (more families in the community where both parents work), and non-support from contemporary educational research. (note 9) Despite the pressures of added requirements and changes in the community, a significant chunk of each day's time has been reserved for Explore Time across the entire history of the program

Explore Time is a time when children can pursue their own investigations and activities in the class. It is a time when the children do things. It is a time the children see as quintessential Multiage. When I asked children how Multiage was different than "the regular" (their term for the self-contained portion of the school), they talked about Multiage being a place "where we do things." Later in the research when I asked them to choose photographs that were typical of what they did in their rooms, they chose photographs showing themselves at work doing things" or work that had been carried out (writings, drawings, paintings, journals, block constructions) during Explore Time. Clearly Explore Time is not free time. It is a time for responsible choice. It is a time where they continue with work begun during activity time, investigate something brought to school and shared during sharing time, or continue working on something they started in an Explore Time earlier in the week or the week before. It is a time to work on something for use later in the day like a costume for a play. It is a time to read a book with a friend in another room. It is a time to play a game in another Multiage room. Regardless of what you do, you must be able to explain it to a teacher or another child when asked. You must be able to articulate just what you are doing, what you are exploring.

Like self-contained classrooms, the moment to moment interactions and activities in this Multiage room are sequenced chronologically. Minutes pass and things happen. One way of keeping track of their occurrence is by a sequential minute to minute count. But this ongoing chronological passage of spending time in an activity is not to be confused with learning time. Learning time is the accumulation of moments that are directed toward learning a particular thing, be it a skill, an attitude, a concept, or a way of being with another human being. Anne sees Explore Time as a period of the day where lots of learning time occurs. It is a time where the interactions of the children with the materials of the classroom and with each other constitutes a rich learning time. It isn't necessarily sequential, but it is rich in its support of children's learning and their learning about what it is to learn. In Explore Time they practice community with one another, they watch other kids at work at things they haven't yet figured out knowing full well their time will come, they have fun with friends constructing something. The Multiage team talks about Explore Time in its interview as almost a way of going to school. I wondered if given their choice, would most of what they did during the day be Explore Time?

"Well, this is a way of going to school which to me isn't all that different other than the fact that you give the children what they feel is some say in what they're doing, their choice kind of thing, and a little bit of independence. I think they need that. Every once and a while I think, 'What have I done in my room that was all that great?' and then I stop and think, 'Well, that was what they needed,' the conversation around the sandbox, and the process (of working in the sand). They don't get that so much any more. The play is done within limits because they know what their limits are without my telling them and therefore it is a very natural comfortable way for these kids to choose something and do it and we have basically very few problems on the whole."

Explore Time exists because it is more natural to give kids a say in what they want to do. It also continues to exist because the teachers see a greater need for it now than they did when the program started. Community life has changed in the world surrounding the school and families seem to be driven more by economic necessity now than they were when Multiage began.

". . . children coming into school today by and large are different. I think day care has got a lot to do with it. Kids come to school that have been with little kids their own age since they were six months old and very often they are struggling to survive in a social setting before they are ready to. They don't come as secure with their own person as they used to where they were able to be nurtured for a longer time by their parents. And the materialistic side of the parents sort of compensating for their not being there. It is very subtle, but the longer it goes on I think the more obvious it is when compared with the first ten years, with themselves, their space, their position in the group."

Explore Time exists because the teachers see the children as needing time together, time that is structured a different way, time to learn and practice what it means to be a member of a natural,

"Explore Time provides an environment that is rich in learning as well as social interaction and developing responsibility for self and others."

multiage group. And, Explore Time continues to occupy a significant portion of the day because the teachers know it provides a rich context for learning the work of school yet to come for some of the younger children. Explore Time provides an environment that is rich in learning as well as social interaction and developing responsibility for self and others. It is a time for strengthening and appreciating the multiplicity of intelligences in the room.

Anne, often observes a kind of learning during Explore Time that she calls priming the pump and she understands this pump priming as a kind of critical and safe rehearsal for learnings to come. This learning is missing in the lives of children in most conventional school settings. The importance of this learning by eavesdropping that occurs frequently during Explore Time is fundamental in her conviction that a multiage environment is the proper placement for most children in school. It is a safe place to move from the known to the unknown. It is safe because it's okay to watch and it is safe because there are plenty of different models of how to learn available in the classroom environment.

Q: Why is it so hard to shift schooling arrangements to reflect more of a multiage philosophy?

A: Multiage classroom settings are once again being advanced as one solution to the growing divergence between achievers and non-achievers in our public schools. Having done this study, I am compelled to comment on the propriety of using multiage settings to address these issues of achievement.

By itself, creating multiage classroom groupings will not accomplish any ends related to addressing issues of diverging achievement levels in our schools. The teachers involved in such groupings must be able to make alterations of teaching style like those described in The Classroom Study and The Writing Project. This is critical given the tendency of policy makers to address issues of (1) diverging achievers, or (2) uneven class sizes for grade-level groupings by resorting to the imposition of multiage groupings.

Using the diversity of children's learning styles and abilities to make better classroom learning environments has not been the traditional practice in the United States. Part of the reason has been a historical mindset that places a high value on individual accomplishment.

America is a relatively young society. We are nearing the100th anniversary of the ending of the American frontier. The frontier ethic remains a powerful symbol for our nation. Included in this symbolism is the vision of a strong, willful individual, usually male, conquering the odds that nature set before him, winning at all costs. Only the most able and strongest conquered the frontier. These individuals fought and persevered their way to success.

This "ethic" connotes the idea of one set of abilities rising above all others to enable the final victory. We carry with us this implicit acknowledgment that one set of abilities is a goal to which we must all aspire. Our schools are organized to reward a rather narrow set of abilities. Our country continually struggles with the notion that diversity in ability is a good thing. Yet the teachers who succeed in multiage settings teach in a way that honors and uses the diversity of abilities present in their classroom to promote learning. They see their classroom worlds as having many frontiers of learning and they know that all kinds of abilities will be necessary to work on those frontiers. The teaching dispositions the writers identify and the characteristics of the learning environment that describe Room A define this new frontier. To claim that merely grouping children of different ages together in our schools will address the issues we have of differential achievement is to create an unhealthy situation for teachers who are not ready either by disposition or inclination to use the diverse nature of their learners effectively.

Q: What do you think about the usefulness of your research? Will anyone be better off for your having done it?

A: I would hope so. The elements of multiage teaching and learning from Room A and the characteristics identified by the writers are differences of perspective. I would hope the reader might see their interaction as a way of thinking about his or her own practice within the common value of responsiveness to children as learners.

The stories seem to connect well with what teachers know as teaching. Seeing the adjustment of more conventional and well-known teaching procedures to serve a particular vision of learning may be illuminating for some readers. Our stories and descriptions may be particularly useful for preservice students to create a vision of what their classrooms might become as they gain experience with the more procedural aspects of the profession.

I would also hope the justification inherent in Vygotsky's emphasis on learning as a social transaction strengthens our resolve to address fundamental issues of equity in our schools through the use of mixed ability groupings and how we teach them. This research gives us several good indications of what these settings might look like. They are not mixed ability class settings grouped by ability for reading and mathematics.

Finally, the model of multiage teaching that emerged from the study, augmented by the teacher portraits, may provide maps for changing practice for teachers ready to start the journey.

"By itself, creating multiage classroom groupings will not accomplish any ends related to addressing issues of diverging achievement levels in our schools."

169

Q: Will any multiage grouping of children work as well as another?

A: Absolutely not. These writers advocated control over the diversity in their rooms. The Multiage team grouped their children as a team. They knew the children in their unit well and intentionally set up classroom combinations they felt would work well together. This is quite different than saying any diverse grouping of children is better and more workable than a grouping that is less diverse. The key is reaching an intentional balance in the student groupings on several dimensions, achievement being only one of them.

Q: Will a "multiage style" work in a single grade classroom?

A: To a degree. A multiage setting is different than a single grade setting even thought the teaching practices look similar. The research didn't address this issue but my conversations with the children of Room A lead me to believe that they would see their learning quite differently if they were in a room with children of mostly the same age. First of all, their behavior would be different. A room full of similarly aged children magnifies the distinctive and unhelpful aspects of a given developmental level and requires therefore a stronger disciplinary structure from the teacher. The discipline is accomplished through intense management of curriculum or more authoritarian disciplinary procedures.

Secondly, there would be more comparison of who is where, more value put on who is where, and therefore more competition inherent in the setting. The behavior and competition would change the supportive balance in the room and I think the change would be in a less supportive direction. I believe the children would say differential achievement doesn't make much difference in the multiage setting because "everyone is kind of all over the place anyway." In a room where "same-ageism" implies a value for similar achievement standards for all, the reward structures would make a difference to the children. This issue is fundamental to the function of school in a democracy. Is school to sort children on the basis of competition and achievement (its own special frontier?) or is the function of school to allow children to seek their own potential limits of learning in an academically and socially supportive environment?

Q: Anyone can teach multiage, right?

A: Probably not. I have learned through my association with the teacher-collaborators in this research that six preconditions are necessary: the teacher must believe children can take responsibility for their own learning; the teacher must know how to provision a classroom for children who want to learn; resources must be available, thought not as many as teachers sometimes presuppose; tasks of classroom management and organization should be second nature to the teacher; and, the teacher must see him or herself as learner as well as teacher in the classroom environment. If these five conditions are present, only one more is needed. The desire to do it.

And finally. . .

The writers in this study felt a certain obligation to tell their stories because they know their kind of teaching works for many children, many different children. The stories of Jake, Kevin and Silas told about three of those children. Other stories could not be told because Vermont is a small state. To write about them would risk their confidentiality. Their identities remain unknown. But they too, learned. The question this research leaves with us all is simply this: if them, why not all?

"The key is reaching an intentional balance in the student groupings on several dimensions, achievement being only one of them."

171

References

Bruner, J. *Actual Minds, Possible Worlds.* Cambridge, MA: Harvard University Press, 1986.

Bogdan, R. C., & Biklen, S. K. *Qualitative Research for Education.* Boston: Allyn and Bacon, Inc., 1982.

Cohen, E. *Designing Groupwork.* New York: Teachers College Press, 1986.

Coles, Robert. *The Call of Stories: Teaching and the Moral Imagination.* Boston: Houghton Mifflin, 1989.

Denzin, N. K. *Interpretive Interactionism.* Newbury Park, CA: Sage Publications, Inc., 1989.

Dreyfus, S.E. & Dreyfus, H.L. *A Five-Stage Model of the Mental Activities Involved in Direct Skill Acquisition. In P. Benner. From Novice to Expert: Excellence and Power in Clinical Nursing Practice.* Menlo Park, CA: Addison Wesley Publishers, 1980.

Dyson, A.H. *Multiple Worlds of Child Writers: Friends Learning to Write.* New York: Teachers College Press, 1989.

Fantini, M. & Weinstein, G. *The Disadvantaged: Challenge to Education.* New York: Harper and Row, 1968.

Featherstone, J. *Schools Where Children Learn.* New York: Liveright, 1971.

Greene, M. *Quality in Teacher Education.* Paper presented at the meeting of The Holmes Group: Ann Arbor, MI, 1988.

Hughes, Langston. "Dreams." In D. Silver, (ed.), *Make a Joyful Sound: Poems for Children by African-American Poets.* New York: Checkerboard Press, 1990.

Hunt, D.E. *Matching Models in Education.* Toronto: Institute for Studies in Education, 1971.

Hunt, J. McV. *Intelligence and Experience.* New York: The Ronald Press Company, 1961.

Johnson, D. & Johnson, R. *Learning Together and Alone.* 3rd Edition. Englewood Cliffs, NJ: Prentice Hall, 1991.

Kounin, J. S. *Discipline and Group Management in Classrooms.* New York: Holt, Rinehart, & Winston, 1970.

Marshall, C. & Rossman, G.B. *Designing Qualitative Research.* Newbury Park, CA: Sage Publications, Inc, 1989.

Miller, B.A. *The Multigrade Classroom: A Resource Handbook for Small, Rural Schools.* Portland, OR: Northwest Regional Educational Laboratory, 1989.

Padilla, R. *HyperQual Software and User's Guide, Version 2.0.* Chandler: Published by the author, 1989.

Rogers, V. *Teaching in the British Primary School.* New York: The Macmillan Company, 1970.

Schniedewind, N. & Davidson, E. *Cooperative Learning, Cooperative Lives.* Dubuque, Iowa: Wm. C. Brown Company, 1987.

Silberman, C.E. *The Open Classroom Reader.* New York: Vintage, 1973.

Strauss, A. & Corbin, J. *Basics of Qualitative Research: Grounded Theory Procedures and Techniques.* Newbury Park, CA: Sage Publications, Inc., 1990.

Vermont State Board of Education. *The Vermont Design for Education.* Montpelier, VT: The Vermont Department of Education, 1968.

Vygotsky, L.S. *Mind in Society: The Development of Higher Psychological Processes.* Translated and Edited by M. Cole, V. John-Steiner, S. Scribner, E. Souberman. Cambridge, MA: Harvard University Press, 1978.

_____. *Thought and Language.* Translated by A. Kozulin. Cambridge, MA: The MIT Press, 1986.

Woods, P. *Inside Schools: Ethnography in Educational Research.* London: Routledge & Kegan Paul, 1986.

Appendix A

The Classroom Study

Methodology

The study of Room A involved forty days of observation and participation and 137 transcriptions of observations and interviews. The content analysis of my descriptive information followed procedures normally used to make sense of qualitative information (Bogden and Biklen, 1982; Marshall and Rossman, 1989; Strauss and Corbin, 1990). My analysis surfaced thirty-two categories of classroom events with over 100 subcategories within the thirty-two. Overall, the research compiled 217 separate data entries from nine data sources accumulating in excess of 500 pages of notes. I used Hyperqual (Padilla, 1989), a computer-based qualitative data analysis program to carry out most of my observational analysis. The technology was very helpful because of limitations of time and space in my work life.

Types of Data Sources

Types of Data.

1. analytic: The source of these data are entries made in my researcher's journal, separate and apart from the data I recorded in Room A. They are reflective comments about my process of research.

2. class: The source of these data are the entries made in Room A as I observed and recorded events and conversations and impressions of the classroom and the school and its various personnel. The "class" notes are really the field log.

3. interview: The source of these data are the interviews I carried out, recorded, and transcribed with children in Room A.

4. journal: The source of these data is the journal notebook that Anne and I kept with each other.

5. microanalysis: The source of these data are the more quantitative recordings I did as part of my field log.

6. talk: The source of these data are the recorded and transcribed conversations amongst the children of Room A.

7. team interview: The source of these data is the transcription of the recorded interview with the Multiage team.

8. writing team . . . : The source of these data are the notes and minutes taken at several of the meetings of the Multiage Writers' Collaborative.

Appendix B

The Classroom Study

Analytical Categories

1.0.0 Researcher's Relationships and Reflections
    1.1.0 child/researcher relationships
    1.2.0 role of researcher
    1.3.0 my reflections
    1.3.1 [behavior ("mis" vs. "off-task)] *
    1.3.2 [folder doodling (defacing)] *
    1.4.0 learning
    1.5.0 time
    1.5.1. time and growth
    1.6.0 tv images
2.0.0 The Classroom Elements of Anne's Room
    2.1.0 continuity
    2.2.0 grouping
    2.3.0 family
    2.4.0 informality
    2.5.0 interaction
    2.6.0 routines
    2.7.0 overlappingness
3.0.0 The Teacher
    3.1.0 the role of teacher
    3.1.1 planning/thinking schema
    3.1.1.1 "the play" as a microcosm of Anne's style
    3.1.1.2 [trade-offs] *
    3.2.0 teacher talk
    3.3.0 teacher/team relationships
    3.4.0 teacher/researcher relationship

4.0.0 The Children
    4.1.0 kid reflections
    4.2.0 role of the children
    4.3.0 special child
    4.3.1 inappropriate behaviors
    4.3.1.1 direct interventions
    4.3.1.2 redirecting
    4.3.1.3 accepting differential limits
5.0.0 "multiage"
    5.1.0 MA unit history
    5.2.0 MA unit organization
    5.3.0 MA as a culture
    5.3.1 Shelburne Context
    5.3.1.1 special events regular
    5.3.1.1.1 Friday morning specials
    5.3.1.1.2 Sing-a-longs
    5.3.1.1.3 Explore Time
    5.3.2.1 special events annual
    5.3.2.1 "the play"
    5.3.2.2 Camp Day
    5.3.2.3 T-Shirt Day

Appendix C

The Classroom Study

Classroom Elements

2.1.0 Continuity:
used to describe instances of connection with past events in the lives of the children thereby creating a familiar and predictable setting for them.

    2.1.1 home to school
    2.1.2 in groupings
    2.1.3 intentionally planning for continuity
    2.1.3.1 follow through
    2.1.4 helpers
    2.1.4.1. parents and former students
    2.1.5 year to year
    2.1.5.1 same activity from one year to the next
    2.1.6 finishing work later
    2.1 7 in skills
    2.1.8 in activities
    2.1.8.1 "the tree"
2.2.0 Grouping:
used to describe the ways in which children gather or are placed together for classroom events.

    2.2.1 reasons for multiage groupings
    2.2.2 related to multiage grouping
    2.2.3 intentional multiage grouping for helping
    2.2.4 intentional grouping/multiage
    2.2.5 intentional multiage-ing
    2.2.6 older teaching younger
    2.2.7 younger chastising older

2.2.8 using older children for procedural information

2.2.9 working with same-age groups

2.2.10 having a friend to share enthusiasm

2.2.11 Explore Time

2.2.12 Anne's informal style

2.2.13 teacher talk

2.2.14 watching and commenting

2.2.15 prodding and using the researcher

2.2.16 individualized behavior in the afternoon

2.2.17 voting on issues

2.2.18 family

2.3.0 Family:

used to describe instances where a "one for all, all for one" attitude was expressed or prevailed in the classroom, thereby creating the basic understanding that "we are all in this together." We work together, we watch out for each other and we recognize our friendships.

(nb: "Family" was a word used by one of the children to describe what the classroom relationships were like for him. I created the category by combining two stacks: "Inclusiveness" and "Mutuality.")

2.3.1 Inclusivesness

Everyone is a part of both the work and fun times. "We do everything together."

2.3.1.1 in teacher talk

2.3.1.2 watching and commenting

2.3.1.3 prodding and using the researcher

2.3.1.4 individualized behavior in the afternoon

2.3.1.5 voting to decide

2.3.1.6 family

2.3.2 Mutuality

We watch out for each other. If one person has to do something, we all do something. One for all and all for one.

2.3.2.1 informing

2.3.2.2 comment on activity

2.3.2.3 helping

2.3.2.4 disciplining each other

2.3.2.5 limits

2.3.2.6 we share all for each other

2.3.2.7 voting

2.4.0 Informality:

used to describe the typical ambience of the classroom.

2.4.1 groupings

2.4 2 sharing content

2.4.3 chatting, acceptance, inclusiveness

2.4.3.1 multiage group strength

2.4.4 sharing time chit-chat

2.4.5 helping, intentional multiage
2.4.6 forgetting and remembering
2.4.7 shared humor
2.4.8 conversational tone
2.4.9 real-life sensitivities
2.4.10 getting out of bounds, reining it in
2.4.11 conversations during Explore Time
2.4.12 argumentative patter in Lego area with third graders
2.4.13 every day housekeeping issues
2.4.14 comfort in sharing all
2.4.15 a time for natural life occurrence
2.4.16 play segments
2.4.17 as life is — we make mistakes — so what?
2.4.18 humor
2.4.19 making relationships

2.5.0 Interaction:

used to describe the variety of encounters the children have with other people, places, and things in the classroom and school.

2.5.1 Explore Time
2.5.2 watching
2.5.3 eavesdropping
2.5.4 play
2.5.5 modeled help
2.5.6 shared enthusiasm
2.5.7 involvement
2.5.8 sharing work
2.5.9 give and take commenting
2.5.10 excited conversation from all
2.5.11 ongoing, active, constant
2.5.12 zone of proximal development
2.5.13 social interaction building the play
2.5.14 disadvantage
2.5.15 anger, multiage

2.6.0 Routines:

used to describe events that occur every day in the classroom with regularity and predictability.

(nb: "Routines" includes four other stacks: the play, lunch count questions, afternoon, and off-task behavior. Off-task behavior was included within the afternoon stack because it occurred most regularly in the afternoon activity. Inappropriate behavior is placed within The Children stack because of the special case of Sally. Otherwise it was minimal.)

2.6.1 opening circle: math questions
2.6.2 lunch count questions
2.6.3 measurement of the day
2.6.4 measure for the day
2.6.5 announcements, opening circle

Notes

Note 1: Peter Woods' description of his "place" during one of his qualitative inquiries describes nicely my "fit" in Anne's school. Peter's words: "My own experiences, for example, have led me to think of the 'involved observer.' I did not take on an accepted role in the institution, though. . . I occasionally helped out with supervisions, took part in activities such as playing chess, umpiring cricket matches, accompanying pupils on community service. . . and above all shared in staffroom life with the teachers. The involvement was in the relationship entered into with staff and pupils, an identification with the educative process, and a willingness to go along with their perceptions of my role. These perceptions incorporated me into the framework of the school."

Note 2: I developed a way of carrying out a detailed analysis of Explore Time, first because of my own curiosity and second, because I needed data that was beyond impressionistic. I visually swept the room every five minutes. During each sweep I recorded what children were doing, what age and gender of children were engaged in the activity, whether the activity had occurred in the previous five minute period, whether children from another room were included in the activity, and whether or not floaters were drifting through the room unattached to any particular activity. In this way I was able to find out how much persistence there was across the different tasks both in terms of the task continuing from moment to moment and the composition of the group participating in the task.

Note 3: Multiage for years has held a Friday morning special. Every Friday morning after sing-a-long, each teacher offers a special activity in her room. Children from all the Multiage rooms can circulate to whatever room they wish to participate in a given teacher's activity. Anne had offered batteries and bulbs as a one-time event in November. It had been such a popular offering then, she decided to resurrect it in the spring as a regular feature of Explore Time for a week or so, depending on how long interest lasted.

Note 4: From time to time, children will not sit down and engage themselves in an activity. The team refers to these children in these moments as floaters. They don't stay put. Rather they float around the room moving from activity to activity.

Note 5: Monday morning journal time follows opening circle every Monday morning. All children, regardless of age, have to write in their journals about something that happened over the weekend. A parent, mother to one of the younger boys, helps out for this twenty to thirty minute period. It is a good time to write. The children fairly brim over with stories from home.

Note 6: The team mentioned these beliefs at various times during my conversation with them. I list them here for convenience. Taken together, they form the fundamental belief system upon which the program still rests. They are clearly shared by all current team members. Indeed, the original members of the team seem to hold them even more strongly.

Note 7: "Overlapping" is a term first used by Kounin (1970) to describe the ability of teachers to deal with more than two things at once. I have adapted the term for use in this study to mean the simultaneous occurrence of classroom elements.

Note 8: Anne's response was that my presence in the room had made her think more about this very issue. As a result, she organized seating at the tables during Monday morning journals and had the children review ways in which they might help each other during this time.

Note 9: Research work carried out in effective schools has denigrated the apparent usefulness of time that is off task or time that appears to be wasted because students are free to choose their activity. The team might counter these assertions by noting that so much of what children do in these schools is work decided upon by others so that time for learning has been all but supplanted by time for achievement.

Additional Multiage Resources:

American Association of School Administrators. *The Nongraded Primary: Making Schools Fit Children.* Arlington, VA: Author, 1992.

Anderson, Robert H., and Pavan, Barbara N. *Nongradedness: Helping it to Happen.* Lancaster, PA: Technomic Press, 1992.

Ellis, Susan, & Whalen, Susan F. *Cooperative Learning: Getting Started.* New York: Scholastic Professional Books, 1990.

Fogarty, Robin. *The Mindful School: How to Integrate the Curricula.* Palatine, IL: Skylight Publishing, Inc, 1991.

Gardner, Howard. *Frames of Mind: The Theory of Multiple Intelligences.* New York: Basic Books, Inc., 1983.

Gayfer, Margaret, ed. *The Multi-Grade Classroom Myth and Reality: A Canadian Study.* Toronto: Canadian Education Association, 1991.

Gaustad, Joan. *Making the Transition from Graded to Nongraded Primary Education.* Oregon School Study Council Bulletin, Vol. 35, Issue (8). Eugene, OR: Oregon School Study Council, 1992.

_____. *Nongraded Education: Mixed-Age, Integrated and Developmentally Appropriate Education for Primary Children.* Oregon School Study Council Bulletin, Vol. 35, Issue 7. Eugene, OR: Oregon School Study Council, 1992.

George, Paul. *How to Untrack Your School.* Alexandria, VA: Association for Supervision and Curriculum Development, 1992.

Goodlad, John I., and Anderson, Robert H. *The Nongraded Elementary School.* New York: Teachers College Press, rev. 1987.

Grant, Jim. *Developmental Education in the 1990's.* Rosemont, NJ: Modern Learning Press, 1991.

_____. *Creating Multiage Primary Classrooms.* Videocassette. Peterborough, NH: Society for Developmental Education, 1993.

_____. *Creating Multiage Primary Classrooms.* Audiocassette. Peterborough, NH: Society for Developmental Education, 1993.

Grant, Jim, and Johnson, Bob. *The Multiage Handbook.* Peterborough, NH: Crystal Springs Books, (In press).

Gutierrez, Roberto, and Slavin, Robert E. *Achievement Effects of the Nongraded Elementary School: A Retrospective Review.* Baltimore, MD: Center for Research on Effective Schooling for Disadvantaged Students, 1992.

Hunter, Madeline. *How to Change to a Nongraded School.* Alexandria, VA: Association for Supervision and Curriculum Development, 1992.

Kasten, Wendy, and Clarke, Barbara. *The Multi-Age Classroom.* Katonah, NY: Richard Owen, 1993.

Katz, Lilian G.; Evangelou, Demetra; and Hartman, Jeanette Allison. *The Case for Mixed-age Grouping in Early Education.* Washington DC: NAEYC, 1990.

Kentucky Department of Education. *Kentucky's Primary School: The Wonder Years.* Frankfort, KY: Author.

Kentucky Education Association and Appalachia Educational Laboratory. *Ungraded Primary Programs: Steps Toward Developmentally Appropriate Instruction.* Frankfort, KY: KEA, 1990.

Kohn, Alfie. *No Contest: The Case Against Competition.* Boston: Houghton Mifflin Company, 1986.

Manitoba Department of Education. *Language Arts Handbook for Primary Teachers in Multigrade Classrooms.* Winnipeg, Man.: Author, 1988.

National Association of Elementary School Principals. *Standards for Quality Elementary and Middle Schools: Kindergarten through Eighth Grade.* Alexandria, VA: Author, rev. 1990.

_____. *Early Childhood Education and the Elementary School Principal.* Alexandria, VA: Author, 1990.

Oakes, Jeannie. *Keeping Track: How Schools Structure Equality.* New Haven: Yale University Press, 1985.

Province of British Columbia Ministry of Education. *Foundation.* Victoria, BC: Author, 1990.

_____. *Our Primary Program: Taking the Pulse.* Victoria, BC: Author, 1990.

_____. *Primary Program Foundation Document.* Victoria, BC: Author, 1990.

_____. *Primary Program Resource.* Victoria, BC: Author, 1990.

_____. *Resource.* Victoria, BC: Author, 1990.

Society For Developmental Education. *The Multiage, Ungraded Continuous Progress School: The Lake George Model.* Peterborough, NH: Author, 1992.

_____. *Multiage Classrooms: The Ungrading of America's Schools.* Peterborough, NH: Author, 1993.

Virginia Education Association and Appalachia Educational Laboratory. *Teaching Combined Grade Classes: Real Problems and Promising Practices.* Charleston, WV: AEL, 1990.

Wheelock, Anne. *Crossing the Tracks: How 'Untracking' Can Save America's Schools.* New York: New Press, 1992.